WITHDRAWN

YOU'LL NEVER LOOK AT THE NEWS THE SAME WAY AGAIN!

METHVEN, NEW ZEALAND

WHAT'S A DAREDEVIL TO DO WHEN THERE'S NOT ENOUGH SNOW ON THE SLOPES? Freestyle snowboarder Jussi Oksanen and a few of his friends flew to an ice field in Methven, New Zealand, to get their fix. Jussi even tackled a 40-foot (12.2-m)-tall "quarter-pipe," with only a pool of frigid water to catch him if he fell.

NATIONAL GEOGRAPHIC KiDS

weird but true!

RIPPED
FROM THE
HEADLINES
3

REAL-LIFE STORIES YOU HAVE TO READ TO BELIEVE

NATIONAL GEOGRAPHIC

WASHINGTON, D.C.

TABLE OF CONTENTS

INTRODUCTION

THINK THE NEWS ISN'T FOR YOU? That only adults need to be in the know? Think again—and get ready for your mind to be blown! *Weird But True!: Ripped From the Headlines 3* is here, and it's better than ever! Just like the first two editions, this volume has all the things you'd expect in a newspaper—world news, sports and science sections, entertainment stories, and more—but with a funky twist. Everything in these pages is factual, but also wild, wacky, and at times out of this world!

Did you know that ants in New York City feast on fast food? That a group of pet mice in Australia shred on custom-built skateboards? Or that there's a "haunted"

MAY THE FROST BE WITH YOU,
PAGE 154

soda machine in Seattle, Washington, U.S.A.? Chock-full of wild and wonderful weird-but-true tales, this book has it all!

Travel the world from the comfort of your home and discover what it's like to Boogie board down a glacier, rappel into an active volcano, or take a spin in a hot-tub car. Think you'll need a break after all that action? Read on to check into an underwater suite at the Palm hotel in Dubai, United Arab Emirates, where you can snooze with the sharks. Or grab your raincoat for a front-row seat to a wet-weather concert in Dresden, Germany.

From animals to athletes, space to space-age technology, these news stories will take you for a walk on the weird side of this wonderful world. Whether you're reading about futuristic space colonies, mummified monks, or exploding art, one thing's for sure—you'll never look at the news the same way again!

CHAPTER 1

WACKY
WORLD
HEADLINES

MA, NO FEET! • HIGH-FLYING DEALS
TEBOARD PATROL! • THERE'S SOMETH
THIS AT HOME! • HOT-ROD HAIRS
DERN MEALS ALTER ANTS' BOD
GIANT GRASSHOPPERS
LIVES ON LAND? •

EXTREME CLOSE-UP, PAGE 24

LOOK, MA, NO FEET!

GELDERN, GERMANY

Mirko Hanßen has turned inline skating on its head—literally! When he first started, he couldn't even do a handstand. But he wasn't satisfied with standard tricks, so he taught himself to skate with his feet in the air. He now practices up to three hours a day in order to master tricky stunts and flips.

SKATEBOARD PATROL!

WHO OFFICER JOEL ZWICKY

WHAT PATROLS HIS BEAT ON A SPECIALLY DESIGNED LONGBOARD OUTFITTED WITH RED AND BLUE FLASHING LIGHTS AND A GREEN BAY POLICE DEPARTMENT LOGO

WHERE GREEN BAY, WISCONSIN, U.S.A.

WHY THIS INNOVATIVE COP HAD ONE GOAL: TO BREAK DOWN THE DISTRUST THAT SOMETIMES EXISTS BETWEEN SKATEBOARDERS AND POLICE. SO HE GRABBED HIS BOARD AND HIT THE STREETS. NOW HE PATROLS NEIGHBORHOODS AND PARKS WHILE INTERACTING WITH THE PEOPLE HE HELPS PROTECT.

NEWS FEED

>>> **SHELBY TOWNSHIP, MICHIGAN, U.S.A.:** POLICE GOT A LITTLE SQUIRRELLY WHILE ASKING THE PUBLIC FOR HELP CATCHING A CROOK WHO STOLE A

HIGH-FLYING DEALS *WING* THROUGH TOWN

SÃO PAULO, BRAZIL

A clothing store took its goods to the people as part of its "truly surprising" ad campaign—by flying decked-out mannequins around city buildings! The mannequins were attached at the neck to drones (remote-control aircraft), which were then flown through downtown São Paulo, advertising the company's big one-day sale to officebound workers and people passing by on the streets below.

PASSENGERS GIVE *STUCK PLANE* A PUSH

SIBERIA, RUSSIA

Passengers rallied to free their stuck airplane by giving it a human-powered push. The landing gear froze when temperatures dipped to minus 62°F (-52°C). More than a dozen passengers left their seats and braved the icy tarmac, pushing on the wings until the aircraft rolled free. They then boarded, and the flight took off as scheduled. Let's hope they had some hot chocolate on board!

1, 2, 3, PUSH!

TRAILER FULL OF NUTS. THEY POSTED A MUG SHOT OF A SQUIRREL ON SOCIAL MEDIA ALONG WITH INFORMATION ABOUT THE CRIME.

VEXING VARMINTS

1

2

3

HITCHIN' A RIDE

SEABECK, WASHINGTON, U.S.A.

A plucky crow decided to take a ride—on the back of a bald eagle. Wildlife photographer Phoo Chan caught the critter in the act as it swooped toward the much larger bird. Crows show little fear of predatory birds like eagles, and are often quick to "mob," or attack, them if they fly too close to their nests—but it appears that this crow settled for a soft landing instead.

CRAFTY **CROWS** HAVE BEEN KNOWN **TO STEAL** FOOD FROM DOG DiSHES.

NEWS FEED

>>> BEAVER DAM, WISCONSIN, U.S.A.: A COUPLE BROUGHT THEIR YOUNG KANGAROO—SWADDLED IN BLANKETS AND STRAPPED INTO A CAR SEAT—

THERE'S SOMETHING FISHY ABOUT THIS MALL

BANGKOK, THAILAND

Government officials scooped up around 3,000 tilapia, carp, and iridescent shark catfish from the basement of an abandoned—and supercreepy—shopping mall. The building's roof caved in ten years before, letting rain fill the lowest floor. With the pond came a serious mosquito problem, so locals stocked the pool with fish in hopes of controlling the biting pests. The sight of thousands of fish in their eerie home drew tourists from around the world. Although the scaly occupants are now gone, the mall will not be restored to its former glory because the battered building is being torn down.

ANCIENT EGYPTiANS RAISED TiLAPIA ON FiSH FARMS.

HORSES USUALLY *SLEEP STANDING UP* BUT WILL TAKE SHORT NAPS LYING ON THE GROUND.

HORSE FALLS AND CAN'T GET UP

ORANGEVALE, CALIFORNIA, U.S.A.

Firefighters are known for rescuing cats from trees, but horses from bathtubs? Not so much. Phantom, a 30-year-old mare, lost her balance while prancing around her feeding trough—which was actually an old bathtub. Her owner, who happened to see the horse fall, called the fire department to get her out. The horse stayed stuck for nearly half an hour before firefighters tilted the tub on its side and pulled Phantom free.

INTO A RESTAURANT. ALTHOUGH IT WASN'T BOUNCING AROUND THE JOINT, THE POLICE WERE CALLED AND THE COUPLE HAD TO LEAVE.

GREAT BLUE HERON PAY ATTENTION TO THE HERON'S BEAK, AND YOU MIGHT SPOT A HAND.

WHAT IS THAT?

Looks can be deceiving, especially when it comes to body art. Check out these extraordinary transformations.

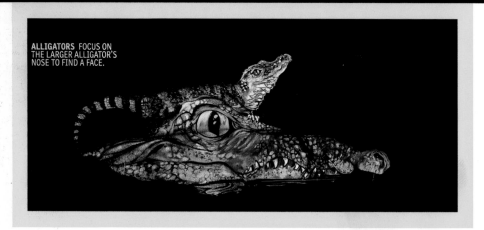

ALLIGATORS FOCUS ON THE LARGER ALLIGATOR'S NOSE TO FIND A FACE.

PEOPLE IN THE **AMAZON** USE THE **JUiCE** FROM THE **JAGUA FRUiT** TO **PAiNT THEiR SKiN.**

ELEPHANT "EYE" SPY A KNUCKLE. DO YOU?

GREAT HORNED OWL FOLLOW THE OWL'S FEET TO FIND A CHIN.

STUNNING
BODY ART
CAN TAKE
12 HOURS
TO CREATE.

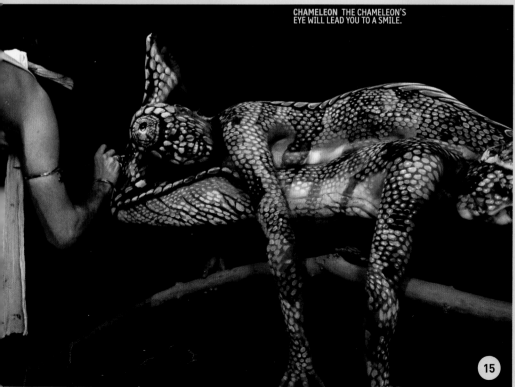

CHAMELEON THE CHAMELEON'S EYE WILL LEAD YOU TO A SMILE.

DO *NOT* TRY THiS
AT HOME!

SKYDIVERS PULL SUPERHERO STUNT

TEUGE, THE NETHERLANDS

ALTHOUGH THESE MEN MAY LOOK LIKE SUPERHEROES ZIPPING THROUGH THE SKIES, THEY'RE ACTUALLY PROFESSIONAL SKYDIVERS. Their winged suits catch the air, allowing the stuntmen to do tricky maneuvers simply by making small adjustments to their body position. Two of the skydivers plummeted toward the ground at 120 miles an hour (193 km/h), while the third did loop-the-loops around them. The special suits allowed the stuntmen to dive at speeds up to 180 miles an hour (290 km/h) and turn at speeds faster than a race car. Such aerial acrobatics are not for amateurs: The team members practiced jumping from airplanes over 8,000 times before attempting this spectacular display.

FASTEST SHOVEL IN THE WEST

WHOOSH!

ANGEL FIRE RESORT, NEW MEXICO, U.S.A.

At the 2015 World Championship Shovel Races, shovels replaced skis as competitors of all ages sailed sled style down the slopes. The fastest racer completed the course in just over 15 seconds, reaching speeds of 65 miles an hour (105 km/h) before crossing the finish line! Who says snow shovels are just for scooping?

MODERN MEALS ALTER ANTS' BODIES

WHO BIOLOGIST CLINT PENICK

WHAT STUDIED CHEMICALS IN PAVEMENT ANTS' BODIES TO LEARN WHAT THEY WERE EATING

WHERE NEW YORK, NEW YORK, U.S.A.

WHY THE FOOD WE EAT CONTAINS CHEMICAL TRACES, OR MARKERS, THAT BECOME PART OF OUR BODIES. PENICK WANTED TO KNOW WHAT ANTS WERE EATING—NATURAL OR FAST FOOD.

OUTCOME PENICK DISCOVERED TRACES OF CORN (FOUND IN NEARLY ALL FAST FOOD) IN THE ANTS, PROVING PAVEMENT ANTS ARE FEASTING ON FAST FOOD LEFTOVERS, RATHER THAN THEIR TRADITIONAL DIET OF INSECTS. THIS MAY BE GOOD FOR US, THOUGH—THE ANTS ARE CLEANING UP OUR MESS!

NEWS FEED

>>> **ATLANTIC OCEAN:** A JACK RUSSELL TERRIER RECENTLY GAINED HIS SEA LEGS BY RACKING UP 20,000 MILES (32,000 KM) SAILING THE ATLANTIC OCEAN ON HIS

HIGH-TECH HOTEL HITS JAPAN

NAGASAKI, JAPAN

Want to rest your head in a tech lover's dream? Henn-na Hotel is the place for you. A face-recognition system captures images of each visitor's face upon check-in. That image acts as a key to open the door to their room. The high-tech hotel is also partially staffed with humanoid robots that chat with visitors while completing tasks ranging from registering guests to cleaning.

THE TOP BANANA

MECCA, CALIFORNIA, U.S.A.

When items from a banana museum went up for sale on eBay, Fred Garbutt bought the whole bunch. His International Banana Museum features nearly 20,000 tidbits honoring the popular yellow fruit. The new top banana even wears a yellow suit and drives around town in his "Banana Bug."

AN A-PEEL-ING NEW MUSEUM

OWNER'S YACHT. NEXT UP, THE FIRST MATE AND HIS SKIPPER ARE SWITCHING GEARS FOR A MOTORCYCLE TRIP THROUGH SCANDINAVIA!

HOT-ROD

YOU HAVE **ABOUT** **100,000** HAIRS ON YOUR HEAD.

SALERNO, ITALY

Italian hairstylist Maria Lucia Mugno decided her car needed a new style—so she covered it with human hair. The project started when Mugno and an assistant began adding hair extensions to the car. They used hair from India for the task, selecting the silky strands for their thickness and strength. It took the pair over 150 hours to stitch the furry covering onto every available surface—leaving only the windows, mirrors, headlights, wheels, and license plate hair-free. The blond, brown, and black—coated car, complete with bangs, earned Mugno the world record for hairiest car in 2010. But that wasn't enough for the trendsetting stylist. Four years later, she added another 44 pounds (20 kg) of hair—by fashioning a massive butterfly out of crimped locks that she attached to the back of the car. According to Mugno, the wings are a symbol of peace and freedom. Or at least the freedom to do as you like to your car.

HUMAN HAIR HAS BEEN USED TO **CLEAN UP** **OIL SPILLS.**

HAIR-STYLIST

BEAUTICIAN DECORATES CAR WITH 265 POUNDS (120 KG) OF HUMAN HAIR

COMBED, CURLED, AND READY FOR A CLOSE-UP!

THAT'S ONE HAIRY RIDE!

FEEJEE MERMAID WOWS THE WORLD

1842

A mummified "mermaid" wowed New York when it was revealed by a scientist—who turned out to work for the famous showman P. T. Barnum. The mermaid was actually a monkey body that had been stitched to a fish tail. The curious creature had supposedly already traveled the world, tricking people from Japan (where it was made) to the Netherlands and England, before making its trip to the Big Apple.

>>> NEW SPECIES HOAXES

1930s

GIANT GRASSHOPPERS INVADE FARMERS' FIELDS

During the Dust Bowl, grasshoppers became farmers' worst nightmare as they attacked crops across the United States. As a fun way of dealing with the ever present pest, people began using trick photography to make pictures and postcards showing humans next to larger-than-life hoppers. Some images used superimposed pictures of grasshoppers on top of smaller-size people; others showed people tackling grasshoppers that were actually statues.

HOW THE JACKALOPE GOT ITS ANTLERS

1932

Taxidermied, or stuffed, rabbits with antlers on their heads are a common sight in the western United States, but the famed jackalope—fake as it is—is based on an actual animal. Rabbits that catch a certain virus grow large knobs on their heads. The knobs aren't really antlers, of course, but they sure look like them. The first official jackalope was a taxidermied rabbit with some deer antlers glued onto its head.

OCTOPUS LIVES ON LAND?

1998

An elaborate website about the plight of the Pacific Northwest tree octopus had people worried about the endangered critter—even though it didn't really exist. The rare octopods supposedly lived in trees, where they caught insects and other small animals and stole eggs from nests. Still tied to water, they returned to streams to lay eggs. The site blamed Sasquatch predators—another mythical creature—and deforestation for their dwindling numbers.

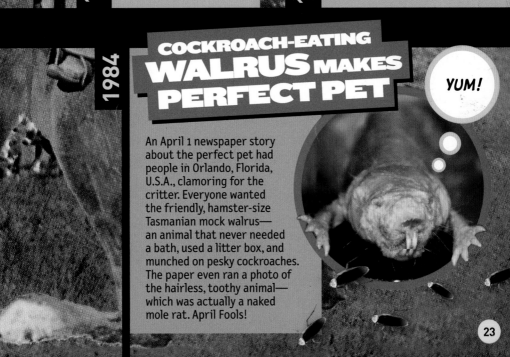

1984

COCKROACH-EATING WALRUS MAKES PERFECT PET

YUM!

An April 1 newspaper story about the perfect pet had people in Orlando, Florida, U.S.A., clamoring for the critter. Everyone wanted the friendly, hamster-size Tasmanian mock walrus— an animal that never needed a bath, used a litter box, and munched on pesky cockroaches. The paper even ran a photo of the hairless, toothy animal— which was actually a naked mole rat. April Fools!

NOW *THAT'S* AN EXTREME CLOSE-UP!

AMBRYM ISLAND, VANUATU

GEORGE KOUROUNIS TOOK SELFIES TO A WHOLE NEW LEVEL WHEN HE RAPPELLED INTO A VOLCANO TO TAKE ONE. The storm chaser and adventurer suited up for the descent into the Marum crater, home to one of the few active lava lakes in the world. A special mask protected Kourounis and three team members from dangerous gases as they rappelled into the crater—a descent equal to dropping down the side of the Empire State Building. Once near the bubbling bowl of molten rock, Kourounis donned a protective heat suit and made the final drop for his famous photo.

ANCIENT
DISCOVERIES

STATUE MASKS MUMMIFIED MONK

ASSEN, THE NETHERLANDS

A gold-painted statue of the Buddha houses a much more valuable find—the mummy of a 1,000-year-old Chinese monk. Someone restoring the statue spotted the mummy through a hole in the bottom. Scientists then took x-ray-like images to peer inside the papier-mâché idol, revealing the seated monk. Researchers believe the monk may have turned himself into a mummy by eating a special diet and drinking poisonous tea to help preserve his tissues.

SOME *EGYPTIAN* MUMMIES WERE STUFFED WITH SAWDUST.

NEWS FEED

TAIWAN: A MAN TRAWLING FOR FISH PULLED AN UNEXPECTED FIND FROM HIS NET: THE JAWBONE OF AN ANCIENT HUMAN. THE BONE, WHICH WAS HAULED IN

MASTODONS STOOD **10** FEET (3 M) AT THE **SHOULDER.**

MAMMOTH BACKYARD FIND

BELLEVUE TOWNSHIP, MICHIGAN, U.S.A.

When two men were digging in a back yard, neither had bones on the brain. But when they unearthed a four-foot (1.2-m)-long rib bone, the men knew they had something huge on their hands. They initially thought the rib belonged to a dinosaur, but after calling in an expert, they learned the rib—and the other 41 bones they uncovered— belonged to a mastodon that lived as long as 14,000 years ago and had likely been killed by primitive people.

THE MAYA ATE CHOCOLATE, GUACAMOLE, AND *SUPER-SPICY* SALSAS.

KITCHEN REMODEL REVEALS MYSTERIOUS MURAL

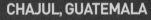

CHAJUL, GUATEMALA

Talk about a trip back in time! A family renovating their home uncovered a 300-year-old Maya mural. As the family chipped layers of plaster from their kitchen wall, spots of color underneath turned out to be a painting depicting a procession of people dressed in both Maya and Spanish clothing—and some appear to be holding human hearts. Scientists are racing to unlock the mural's secrets before it fades away.

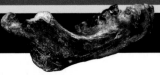

WITH BONES FROM AN EXTINCT SPECIES OF HYENA, IS THE FIRST HUMAN FOSSIL FOUND IN TAIWAN.

TRACING THE SOURCE OF GHOSTLY TRACKS

Feet aren't the only things to leave tracks. Take a look at these intriguing imprints and see if you can identify the source of each one. Answers are at the bottom of the page—no peeking!

1.

A) FLYING SQUIRRELS
B) BIRDS
C) A WOLVERINE

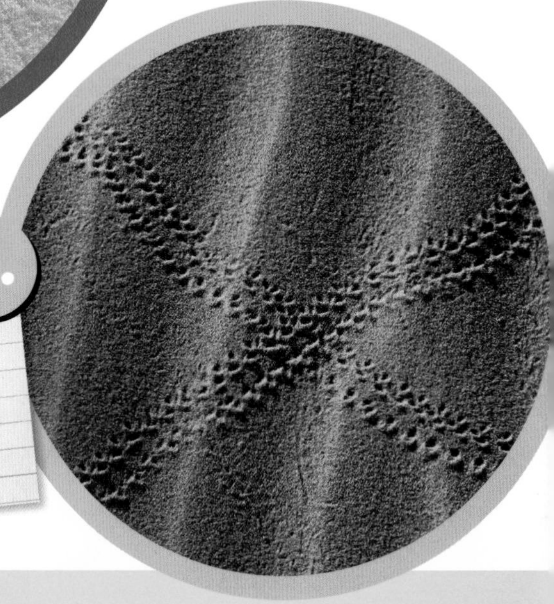

2.

A) A SNAKE
B) MICE
C) A CENTIPEDE

3.

A) A TARANTULA
B) BLOODWORMS
C) A SAND BUBBLER CRAB

4.

A) FIRE ANTS
B) A MOLE
C) AN ENGRAVER BEETLE

5.

A) DRAGONFLIES
B) A STORK
C) SEA TURTLES

CHAPTER 2

WILD ANIMALS

...EAVER IS OUT OF THIS WORLD • NOW THAT'S
...SET • BEES BATTLE OVER HONEY-FILLED HIVE
...Y RESEARCHERS SAVE YOUNG CRANES • THAT
...WALKING, STALKING FROGFISH • SPOOK!
...STUMED CRITTERS • SPLIT

CRAZY COSTUMED
CRITTERS, PAGE 42

INNOVATIVE WAY TO FEED STRAYS

ISTANBUL, TURKEY

Here, boy! A company has created solar-powered kiosks that dispense pet food when plastic bottles are inserted. People are encouraged to pour any remaining water into a dish near the ground before popping the bottle into the bin. Kibble then drops into a food dish to feed the city's massive population of stray cats and dogs. Talk about a win-win!

PET PIG PREVENTS HOME FROM BEING BURGLED

WHO LUDWIG THE POTBELLIED PIG

WHAT PREVENTED BURGLARS FROM ROBBING HIS FAMILY'S HOME BY GROWLING LIKE A DOG

WHERE DERBY, ENGLAND

HOW OWNERS THINK THAT BURGLARS TRYING TO ROB THE HOUSE MUST HAVE WOKEN THE 238-POUND (108-KG) PIG, WHICH THEN GROWLED—A LOUD RUMBLE THAT SOUNDS LIKE A LARGE ROTTWEILER.

OUTCOME THE BURGLARS RAN OFF BEFORE THEY COULD TAKE ANYTHING OF VALUE, AND LUDWIG'S OWNERS PRAISE THEIR PET PIG FOR SAVING THEIR BACON.

NEWS FEED

>>> **LUOHE, CHINA:** VISITORS AT A ZOO IN CHINA WERE SHOCKED WHEN THE "LION" BARKED LIKE A DOG. ON CLOSER INSPECTION, THEY REALIZED THE

FIGHTING **FALCON** *TAKES* *DOWN* **PLANES**

LOS ANGELES, CALIFORNIA, U.S.A.

Don't mess with a mother peregrine falcon. This one directed her talons at remote-control airplanes that ventured too close to her nest. The feisty flier—which can reach speeds of up to 200 miles an hour (322 km/h) when diving—attacked the planes, not stopping until she had knocked them out of the air. Score one for the falcon!

SNEAKY **SPIDER** **EATS** SNAKE

CAIRNS, AUSTRALIA

Tree snakes beware: Golden orb weaver spiders have developed a taste for your kind. One took a tumble into a spider's web and was immediately attacked by the two-inch (5-cm) spinner. After an hour's struggle, the spider succeeded in subduing its slithery supper.

ANIMAL *WAS* A DOG: A HAIRY TIBETAN MASTIFF. IT WASN'T ALONE— ANOTHER DOG WAS FOUND NEARBY POSING AS A WOLF.

SUPERSIZE SOCCER MATCH

LARGEST LAND ANIMAL IS NO MATCH FOR THIS BOY

MOSSEL BAY, SOUTH AFRICA

What's a boy to do when he discovers elephants like to kick a ball around? Challenge them to a soccer match! When five-year-old Finn Johnson visited the Indalu Game Reserve, he and two teens used wooden posts to set up soccer goals and then did their best to keep the ball from the 3.3-ton (3-MT) elephants. "It was a bit scary at first because the elephants were so huge but as soon as I started scoring goals and beating them I wasn't scared anymore," Finn said of the experience. Although the elephants had a clear size advantage, the boys' dribbling skills put them on top in a 3–2 win. The elephants, Shanti and Amari, regularly kick a ball around with their keepers. Doing so gives the animals exercise and gets them used to interacting with people—important preparation for life on the reserve, which brings in daily visitors. Looks like they need a little more time on the practice field!

FINN USES HIS FANCY FOOTWORK TO GET THE BALL FROM HIS OVERSIZE OPPONENT.

ELEPHANTS
CANNOT RUN,
BUT THEY CAN
"SPEED WALK"
AS FAST AS
25 MILES
AN HOUR
(40 KM/H).

ELEPHANTS
ARE
RIGHT-TUSKED
OR
LEFT-TUSKED.

OCEANIC ODDITIES

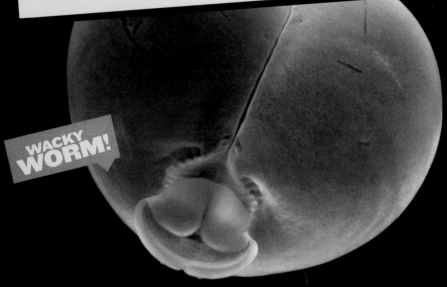

WACKY WORM!

PIG-BUTT WORM PUZZLES SCIENTISTS

PACIFIC OCEAN

One of the weirdest worms known to science doesn't look like a worm at all. The recently discovered—and appropriately named— pig-butt worm looks like, well, a pig's hind end. The worm, which is segmented (sectioned) like other worms, has two sections that inflate like water balloons, flattening nearby segments and giving the curious critter its signature look. The worm drifts about 3,000 feet (914 m) below the ocean's surface, trapping bits of food in a cloud of mucus.

THE **PiG-BUTT WORM** IS ABOUT THE **SiZE** OF A **MARBLE.**

NEWS FEED

>>> **SOUTHERN OCEAN:** ANTARCTIC ICEFISH HAVE CLEAR BLOOD! WITHOUT RED BLOOD CELLS, ICEFISH HAVE FAR LESS OXYGEN IN THEIR BLOOD

WALKING, STALKING FROGFISH

SHALLOW TROPICAL AND SUBTROPICAL WATERS

The hairy frogfish may look like a patch of seaweed, but it's actually a ruthless predator. The fish stakes out a spot where it blends in and then dangles a wormlike lure in front of its mouth. When hungry fish take the bait, the frogfish snaps them up. But the sly predator doesn't always wait for food to come to it. When it spots a fish that looks like easy prey, the frogfish stalks it, walking on its fins until it's close enough to slurp down its meal.

IF THE **FROGFISH'S** "**LURE**" GETS **EATEN**, IT CAN GROW A **NEW ONE**.

BROWNSNOUT SPOOKFISH EYES ARE **SPLiT iN TWO,** WITH **ONE PART LOOKING UP** AND THE **OTHER LOOKING DOWN.**

SPOOKTACULAR SPOOKFISH

DEEP SEA

An extremely rare image in the deep ocean stunned scientists. The smallspine spookfish—which is a relative of sharks—lives 4,600 to 8,500 feet (1,400–2,600 m) below the ocean's surface and uses its large fins to fly through the water. Its oversize eyes help it navigate the dark ocean depths. The ghostly creatures will likely remain a mystery, because their extreme location makes them almost impossible to study.

THAN OTHER FISH, FORCING THEIR HEARTS TO WORK HARDER. GOOD THING THEIR OXYGEN-RICH ENVIRONMENT HELPS THEM MUDDLE THROUGH.

HANDLE WITH CARE

1867

As early as 1867, the United States Postal Service started carrying honeybees! Beekeepers boxed up colonies of bees in containers made from wood. With their queen at the center, the honeymakers buzzed about for the duration of their trip. Mail carriers still deliver boxes of bees, but some aren't wild about their work when the winged wonders arrive at the post office.

JUST DROPPING IN

1948

Troublesome beavers in Idaho were sent to a new location—by parachute. The beavers were packed in specially designed boxes attached to leftover World War II parachutes. Wildlife handlers flew the rodents to a remote area of Idaho and dropped them out of the plane. The boxes opened when they hit the ground, freeing the beavers in their new home.

>>> WACKY ANIMAL TRANSPORTATION

1919

ALL ABOARD!

SQUIRRELS **RUN** IN A **ZIGZAG** PATTERN TO **ESCAPE** PREDATORS.

What are eastern gray squirrels doing in the West Coast state of Oregon? They hitched a ride on a train, of course. A former Oregon governor traveled to the East Coast, where he first spotted the species. He was so fascinated by the squirrels that he had 48 of them shipped across country by train. The squirrels adapted so well to their new home that they now vastly outnumber the western species.

THAT'S NO ORDINARY FLYING FISH!

KING SALMON CAN **WEIGH** **100** POUNDS (45 KG).

2014

It's no easy task to move salmon—which swim upstream to lay eggs—around river-blocking dams. But a new vacuum-driven tube dubbed the "salmon cannon" makes the trip as easy as a flick of the fins. The contraption sucks up fish at the base of the dam and flings them right over the top. Fish fly from the end of the cannon and into the water on the other side, overcoming the oversize obstacle in a matter of seconds.

CRAFTY RESEARCHERS SAVE YOUNG CRANES

2001

Whooping cranes are migratory birds, but without adults to show them the way, young birds won't travel. Wildlife scientists rearing endangered whooping crane chicks decided to play adult and guide the young birds by ultralight airplane. The researchers played engine sounds to incubating eggs, so when the hatched birds were old enough to migrate, they readily followed the small plane that guided them along their route.

WEAVER
IS OUT OF THIS WORLD

QUEENSLAND, AUSTRALIA

THOSE BLACK EYES PEERING OUT FROM BETWEEN THE LEAVES DON'T BELONG TO AN ALIEN. In fact, they're not eyes at all. The dark spots decorate the hind end of a green orb weaver spider, also known as the "alien-butt" spider. Those eerie "eyes" can stop predators in their tracks, giving the spider a few seconds to scurry to safety. Their location in the rear helps, too. Even if a critter tried to take a nip, essential parts of the spider's body—including its head—would remain unharmed.

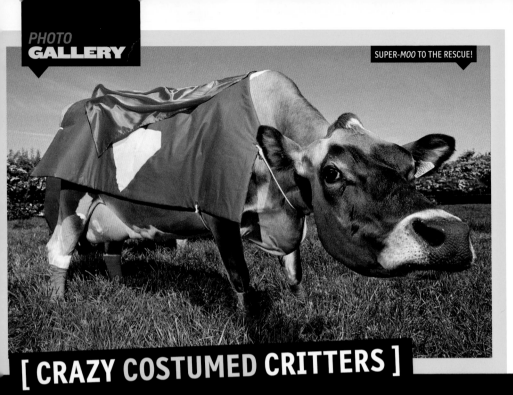

SUPER-*MOO* TO THE RESCUE!

[CRAZY COSTUMED CRITTERS]

People aren't the only ones who like to add a little fun to their look. These pets are rocking some seriously swanky threads.

TURTLE IS READY FOR TAKEOFF.

POPULAR HALLOWEEN **PET COSTUMES** ARE **DEVILS,** PUMPKINS, AND **PRINCESSES.**

THAT'S NOT A FROG—IT'S A PRAIRIE DOG!

MINNIE PIG POSES FOR THE CAMERA.

IN **2012** IN
ST. LOUIS, MISSOURI, U.S.A.,
1,326 DOGS
DONNED
COSTUMES FOR A
GIANT PARADE.

THIS CAT HAS *MEOW*-VELOUS STYLE.

NOW THAT'S A STARRY-EYED GAZE

SYLMAR, CALIFORNIA, U.S.A.

Zeus, a Western screech-owl, has eyes that look like a starry night. His rescuers think damage from an injury created the starry look and also left him nearly blind, so Zeus can't be released into the wild. Instead, the adorable raptor lives at a wildlife center, where happy helpers give him his daily mouse meal.

BEES BATTLE OVER HONEY-FILLED HIVE

WHO SUGARBAG BEES

WHAT WAGED WAR OVER A HONEY-FILLED HIVE

WHERE BRISBANE, AUSTRALIA

WHY TO TAKE CONTROL OF THE HIVE AND INSTALL THEIR QUEEN.

HOW ONE SPECIES OF TINY, STINGLESS BEE LAUNCHED A BLITZ ATTACK AGAINST ANOTHER, SWARMING THEIR HIVE AND DRAGGING THE DEFENDERS FROM THEIR HOME.

OUTCOME AFTER WEEKS OF FIGHTING, SCIENTISTS ANALYZED THE BEES' DNA TO LEARN THAT THE ATTACKING COLONY HAD SUCCEEDED IN THEIR TAKEOVER ATTEMPT, USURPING THE THRONE—AND LIQUID TREASURE—FOR THEIR QUEEN.

NEWS FEED

>>> **TAMBOPATA, PERU:** MYSTERIOUS GLOWING DOTS IN THE AMAZON RAIN FOREST TURNED OUT TO BE PREDATORY GLOWWORMS. THE BEETLE

WILD MONKEY CRADLES KITTEN

BALI, INDONESIA

Who said pets are just for people? This long-tailed macaque adopted an abandoned ginger kitten, which it cuddles and snuggles in the forest of Indonesia. The macaque belongs to one of five troops in the Sacred Monkey Forest Sanctuary, an area set aside to protect the monkeys—which in turn protects this furry pet.

AW!

SAY CHEESE!

TIAN SHAN MOUNTAINS, CHINA

This cuddly critter, called an Ili pika, blends beautifully into its rocky habitat, making it tough to spot. In fact, it's only the 29th ever seen—and scientists have spent two decades searching. The man who originally discovered the pika finally managed to snap a few photos of the elusive animal, which he hopes to protect from extinction.

LARVAE POKE THEIR HEADS OUT OF THEIR BURROWS, WAITING FOR PREY TO SPOT THE GLOW AND WANDER CLOSE ENOUGH TO NAB.

SPLiT
DOWN THE MiDDLE

RICHARDSON, TEXAS, U.S.A.

CARDINALS ARE HARD TO MISS WITH THEIR BRIGHT RED FEATHERS, AND EVEN FEMALES GRAB ATTENTION WITH THEIR ORANGEY BEAKS. BUT THIS BIRD STOOD OUT BECAUSE IT WASN'T MALE OR FEMALE—IT WAS BOTH! The right side of the bird's body has the coloring of a female and the left side that of a male, a rare condition that has also been reported in butterflies and lobsters. Math professor and amateur photographer Larry Ammann spotted the double-sexed bird at his feeder and caught a few quick pics. Ammann says he has not heard the bird sing like a male or chirp like a female. But the lucky bird did make it big—it was featured on an episode of the game show *Jeopardy!*

HiDE-AND-SEEK

Nature's crawling with critters that use camouflage to stay hidden in plain sight. See if you can spot the camouflaged critters in these photos. Answers are at the bottom of the page.

1.

2.

CHAPTER 3

INCREDIBLE
INVENTIONS

T YOUR SUITCASE CARRY YOU! • ROVING, ROLLING R
PERHUMAN SPEED • LET THE STARS GUIDE YOUR
NKS AFTER ONE TRY • PORTABLE PAMPERING • PRO
RM INTO A SMARTPHONE • MILK STRAIGHT FROM
UR THOUGHTS • GIANT ROBOTS STOP TRAFFIC • U

**HEAR THE CITY
AS NEVER BEFORE,**
PAGE 53

LET YOUR SUITCASE CARRY YOU!

CHANGSHA, CHINA

Tired of hauling heavy luggage? So was Chinese inventor He Liangcai. He created a battery-powered suitcase scooter that not only motorizes your stuff, but also carries up to two people. It took Liangcai ten years to develop the scootercase, which tops out at 12 miles an hour (19 km/h). Forget running to catch your plane—just sit back and enjoy the ride!

ROVING, ROLLING ROBOT

WHO INVENTORS AT GUARDBOT

WHAT BUILT A BALL-SHAPED ROBOT THAT PATROLS ON LAND OR IN THE WATER. PEOPLE CONTROL THE ROBOT FROM AFAR,
USING VIDEO FROM THE ROBOT'S CAMERAS TO KEEP AN EYE ON THE SURROUNDING AREA.

WHERE STAMFORD, CONNECTICUT, U.S.A.

WHY INVENTORS ORIGINALLY DESIGNED THE ROLLING ROBOT
FOR A MISSION TO MARS, BUT ITS ABILITY TO POWER OVER SNOW, WATER, SAND, AND UNEVEN GROUND ALSO MAKES IT PERFECT FOR SAFETY PATROLS. CAMERAS HOUSED IN THE BUBBLE-LIKE DOMES SEND VIDEO AND INFORMATION ABOUT SUSPICIOUS OBJECTS TO OFF-SITE CONTROLLERS.

NEWS FEED

 RAMAT GAN, ISRAEL: RESEARCHERS ARE CREATING DNA "NANOROBOTS" THAT CAN BE INJECTED INTO CANCER PATIENTS. THE TINY BOTS CRUISE

BEEHIVE BUZZ

NEW SOUTH WALES, AUSTRALIA

Honey lovers rejoice! The Flow hive allows beekeepers to collect hive-fresh honey in a matter of minutes. The keepers can drain honey from the specially designed frames without disturbing the bees hanging out inside the hive. By not removing frames to get honey, the Flow hive reduces a messy, hours-long process to a tidy 20 minutes!

HEAR THE CITY
AS NEVER BEFORE

GATESHEAD, ENGLAND

Popular tourist destinations have dozens of ways people can take in the city's sights, but with Binaudios, people can listen to its sounds instead! When users point the Binaudios—which were modeled after binoculars—at a specific spot, the device plays sounds that were recorded there.

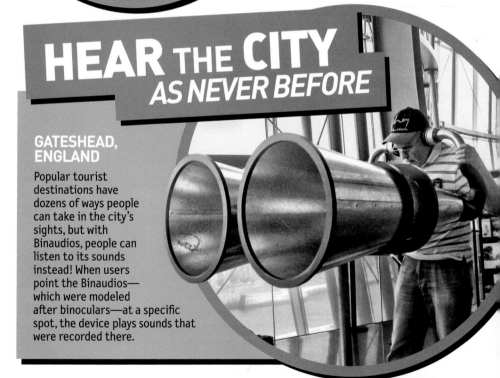

THROUGH THE BODY IN SEARCH OF CANCER CELLS. WHEN THEY ENCOUNTER ONE, THEY RELEASE ANTICANCER DRUGS TO DESTROY IT!

RACING TOWARD

SUPERHUMAN

SPEED

SAN FRANCISCO, CALIFORNIA, U.S.A.

INSPIRATION STRIKES AT THE ODDEST TIMES, AND IN THIS CASE IT HIT KEAHI SEYMOUR WHILE HE WAS WATCHING A TV SHOW ABOUT KANGAROOS WHEN HE WAS 12. Seymour later went on to study the legs of ostriches, racehorses, cheetahs, and greyhounds before building a pair of boots that helped him leap like a long-legged animal. The Bionic Boots mimic the springlike action of an animal's leg. For his first pair, Seymour used some old Rollerblades (minus the wheels), steel tubing, and bungee cords. He has since redesigned the boots, making them lighter and faster. The new and improved Bionic Boots are made from lightweight carbon fiber (the same stuff used to make race cars and airplanes), with rubber speargun tubing to add a bigger bounce. The extra oomph allows him to easily achieve a speed of 15 miles an hour (24 km/h) over rocky, uneven terrain—even leaping over small shrubs that get in his way. In full sprint, Seymour can reach an astounding 25 miles an hour (40 km/h), but he's still not satisfied with that speed. "Eventually," he says, "I'd like to run as fast as an ostrich at 45 miles an hour (72 km/h)."

OTOTO (LONDON, ENGLAND) A SIMPLE OTOTO KIT CAN TURN ANYTHING INTO A MUSICAL INSTRUMENT. EVEN VEGGIES!

[MYSTIFYING MUSICAL INSTRUMENTS]

Sure, you may know all the instruments in the orchestra, but that doesn't mean you know all the music makers out there! Check out these wacky musical wonders.

THE **OLDEST MUSICAL INSTRUMENTS—** FLUTES MADE FROM **BIRD BONES—** ARE MORE THAN **40,000** YEARS OLD.

EARTH HARP (MALIBU, CALIFORNIA, U.S.A.) THE STRINGS OF THIS HARP CAN STRETCH ACROSS A VALLEY OR TO THE TOP OF A TALL BUILDING, TURNING ANYTHING ON EARTH INTO MUSIC.

SINGING TESLA COILS (AUSTIN, TEXAS, U.S.A.) BAND ARCATTACK USES THE ELECTRICITY BURSTING FROM TESLA COILS TO CREATE AN EXPLOSIVE MUSICAL EXPERIENCE.

ALPHASPHERE (BRISTOL, ENGLAND) THIS BALL ISN'T FOR KICKING AROUND A FIELD—IT'S FOR JAMMING! PLAYERS PUSH TOUCH PADS AND ROCK OUT TO MUSIC OF THEIR OWN DESIGN.

THE TWO-STRING VIOLIN BELOW WAS PRINTED ON A 3-D PRINTER.

PIEZOELECTRIC VIOLIN (NORTH MIAMI BEACH, FLORIDA, U.S.A.) NO, IT'S NOT A WEAPON. IT'S A FUTURISTIC VIOLIN THAT FEATURES JUST TWO STRINGS.

LET THE
STARS
GUiDE YOUR RiDE

ARTIST CREATES SOLAR-POWERED CYCLE PATH

NUENEN, THE NETHERLANDS

CYCLISTS IN THE NETHERLANDS CAN NOW ENJOY A STARRY RIDE, NO MATTER THE WEATHER. Artist Daan Roosegaarde patterned this popular new bike path after Dutch painter Vincent van Gogh's famous painting, "The Starry Night." To create the spectacular swirls, Roosegaarde embedded blue and green chips along the pathway. The chips contain tiny LED lights that charge up in sunlight. When the sun sets, they glow, creating nearly half a mile (0.8 km) of glimmering galaxies. The otherwise dark path illuminates cyclists from below with an eerie green light, giving riders a truly sensational spin. Bet your local bike path can't top that.

PARENTS— CAGE YOUR BABIES!

1930s

Baby needs some fresh air? No problem! Simply install your baby cage and stick the infant out the window. The Chelsea Baby Club in London gave these baby cages to its members. For the next few years, the wacky contraptions could be seen clamped onto windows around the city. They even came with curtains, in case the little tyke needed a nap.

PARENTS USED TO SPREAD **LARD**—OTHERWISE KNOWN AS **PIG FAT**—ON THEIR **BABIES' BOTTOMS** TO PREVENT **DIAPER RASH.**

>>> WACKIEST INVENTIONS THROUGH THE YEARS

1960

SMELL-O-VISION TANKS AFTER ONE TRY

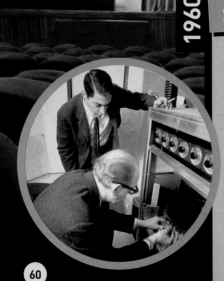

Mike Todd, Jr., created Smell-O-Vision, the first (but not last) attempt to bring scents to movies. His odor-rific invention required specially equipped theaters with pipes running to each seat. As the film reel played, scents matching the scene traveled from a contraption in the lobby to the moviegoers' noses. His idea worked—too well. Viewers complained that the odors mixed in unpleasant ways, making Smell-O-Vision a little too rank to repeat.

THE **AIR** IN SAUNAS CAN REACH **185°F** (85°C).

PORTABLE PAMPERING

1962

Folks from Finland take their saunas seriously—so much so that they invented saunas they could take with them when they traveled. People sit on a built-in seat and zip themselves inside the scaled-down spas, which trap heat close to the body. Holes in the front allow the hands to move freely, so users can read while they relax. The saunas became so popular that Finland's Olympic team reportedly still uses them when they travel.

PHONE FINGER FAIL

2007

An Austrian invented these roll-on finger covers to keep people from smudging their smartphones. The Phone Fingers, which were made of latex, allowed users to swipe, type, and resize—all while maintaining a streak-free screen. The weird wraps worked, but not enough people wanted to wear them on their fingers while out and about, making the doodad a fast flop.

1999

DON'T I LOOK LOVELY?

HARMLESS BEAUTY OR EVIL VILLAIN?

This mask may look like it belongs in a scary movie, but it was actually invented for people who want to recapture their youth. The battery-powered mask zaps muscles with low levels of electricity that make the muscles contract, toning and tightening the face. The inventor says it does for the face what eight sit-ups a second will do for the abs. Sounds frightening, but perhaps the weirdest thing: The bizarre beautifiers are still around!

WACKY WEARABLES

BZZZZZ!

"SEE" WITH YOUR SNEAKERS

RÍO GALLEGOS, ARGENTINA

A college student designed shoes that help blind people sense obstacles around them. Ultrasound sensors housed in the sole of each shoe detect objects up to 25 inches (63.5 cm) away. The shoes send out ultrasound pulses that bounce off objects and return to the sensor. When the wearer nears an object, parts of the shoe vibrate: the toe for an object in front, the sole for an obstacle on the side, and the heel for one in back. The inventor hopes the shoes will make it easier for the blind to find their way around, no matter where in the world they go!

ENGINEERS HAVE **CREATED** A **BiONIC EYE** THAT, WHEN IMPLANTED, LETS SOME **BLiND PEOPLE** SEE SHAPES AND **MOVEMENT.**

NEWS FEED

>>> MUNICH, GERMANY: DASH EARPHONES DO MUCH MORE THAN DELIVER SOUND. THE WIRELESS EARBUDS ALSO STORE MUSIC AND MONITOR MOVEMENT—

TURN YOUR ARM INTO A SMARTPHONE

PARIS, FRANCE

Can't reach your phone? Researchers are working on the Cicret Bracelet, which will project your phone screen onto your arm with a flick of the wrist. The movement triggers a tiny "pico projector" inside the bracelet, which casts the screen onto the skin. Light-beam technology allows wearers to tap, scroll, and type on their arms, just as they would on their phone screens, by telling the processor where the finger is located and what it's doing. The device is even waterproof, so you can answer your phone in the pool.

THE FIRST **TOUCHSCREENS, DEVELOPED** IN THE **1960s,** WERE USED BY **AIR-TRAFFIC** CONTROLLERS.

ON AVERAGE, PEOPLE AROUND THE WORLD **SiT** FOR **9.3** HOURS PER DAY.

GO AHEAD, TAKE A SEAT!

RÜTI, SWITZERLAND

Not sure if you'll need to sit or stand? Take along a Chairless Chair. The lightweight frame fits against the back of the legs and is held in place with a series of belts that secure it to your body. The gadget moves with you, allowing you to walk, climb stairs, and even run normally. When you're ready to take a seat, simply shift into a sitting position, press a button, and presto! The innovative invention stiffens, allowing you to sit back and relax anytime and anywhere.

ALLOWING USERS TO TRACK THEIR ACTIVITY. YOU CAN EVEN ANSWER YOUR CELL PHONE WITH A TAP OF YOUR FINGER.

MiLK
STRAiGHT
FROM THE COW

THE MILK THAT ALAN HEWSON AND HIS CATTLE PRODUCE IS SIMPLY *MOO-VELOUS!*

COWS **DRINK** ENOUGH **WATER** EVERY DAY TO FILL A **BATHTUB.**

A TYPICAL **DAIRY COW** PRODUCES **104** **GLASSES** OF **MILK** A DAY.

VENDING MACHINE OFFERS CUSTOMERS COW-FRESH MILK

EASTWELL, LEICESTERSHIRE, ENGLAND

Visitors to a farm in rural England can get the world's freshest milk—from a vending machine! Crossroads Farm may be known for its cheese, but when farmers Jane and Alan Hewson went looking for a way to use the extra milk they had from their herd, they came up with a smash hit. They installed the unconventional vending machine to offer passersby the freshest milk possible. The creamy liquid is pumped from one of their 60 red poll dairy cows just a few feet from where customers fill their bottles. Don't worry, the cow-fresh milk is pasteurized to kill any bacteria before being transferred to a container inside the contraption. Visitors pay about $1.50 for a quart (1 L) of the stuff, which is so fresh you can spoon the cream off the top. The Hewsons were surprised by the success of their out-of-the-way offering, which spread by word of mouth: As many as 30 people a day popped in for the creamy concoction just a month after the machine was installed.

COMFORT KITTY FROM AFAR

MINNEAPOLIS, MINNESOTA, U.S.A.

People who miss their pets when they're away from home can talk to their furry friends using PetChatz. The gizmo is attached to the wall at pet-eye level, where cats and dogs can see and hear their owners on the screen. Owners can even give treats and fill the room with "soothing" scents for their homebound critters.

HELMET READS YOUR THOUGHTS

WHO AISTE NOREIKAITE

WHAT CREATED THE EXPERIENCE HELMET, A MODIFIED MOTORCYCLE HELMET THAT TURNS BRAIN SIGNALS INTO SOUND

WHERE LONDON, ENGLAND

WHY NOREIKAITE IS INTERESTED IN MEDITATION—THE PRACTICE OF FOCUSING ON THE PRESENT MOMENT—AND THOUGHT THAT LISTENING TO THE BRAIN'S ACTIVITY AS ELECTRONIC MUSIC MIGHT HELP PEOPLE MEDITATE MORE EASILY. JUST IMAGINE LISTENING TO YOUR OWN PERSONAL SOUNDTRACK AS YOU KICK BACK AND RELAX.

NEWS FEED

>>> LAUSANNE, SWITZERLAND: THEY DON'T GIVE YOU X-RAY VISION, BUT THE LATEST CONTACT LENSES MAGNIFY WITH THE WINK OF AN EYE! THE LENSES, WHICH

WOULD YOU LIKE KETCHUP WITH YOUR FRIES?

SUFFOLK, ENGLAND

Fire up the fryer: Gardeners who love fries with ketchup are flocking to the new Ketchup 'n' Fries plant. The wacky creation—which is designed by joining the stems of potato and tomato plants and then allowing them to grow together—produces hundreds of cherry tomatoes on top and potatoes underground. That's one delicious bounty!

GIANT ROBOTS STOP TRAFFIC

KINSHASA, DEMOCRATIC REPUBLIC OF THE CONGO

The capital city had traffic troubles, with too many cars and pedestrians competing for space on the crowded streets. Instead of installing more traffic lights, a group of female engineers set up eight-foot (2.5-m)-tall solar-powered robots to regulate the flow. It's working pretty well, possibly because when a giant robot tells you to stop, you listen.

CONTAIN TINY MIRRORS THAT MAKE NEARBY OBJECTS APPEAR LARGER, MAY EVENTUALLY HELP PEOPLE WITH FAILING VISION TO SEE BETTER.

FUTURISTIC FRAMES

Glasses might make a fashion statement, but these lensed inventions create a whole new experience for the wearer. Can you match the wacky glasses to their function? Answers are at the bottom of the page.

1.

2.

A. TOO LAZY TO LIFT YOUR HEAD? THESE SPECS LET THE WEARER READ WITHOUT HAVING TO SIT UP.

B. HEAVY-DUTY SUN PROTECTION LETS PEOPLE WHO CAN ONLY SEE IN THE DARK ENJOY A SUNNY DAY.

C. CAN'T SEE CLEARLY? SIMPLY ADJUST THE PRESCRIPTION WITH A TWEAK OF THE LENS.

3.

4.

5.

D. THESE GLASSES SHOW BLIND PEOPLE WHAT'S IN FRONT OF THEM BY SENDING SIGNALS TO AN UNLIKELY BODY PART.

E. OUT-OF-THIS-WORLD ANIMATIONS TAKE THE WEARER ON A 3-D TOUR OF OTHER PLACES.

F. NEED DIRECTIONS? THESE FUTURISTIC FRAMES WILL LEAD THE WAY.

FREAKY FOOD

CREEPY CAKES, PAGE 82

71

WACKY MOLDS GROW FUN FRUIT

OH, BABY!

CHINA

What's a better snack than fresh fruit? Fruit in fun shapes! In Japan and China, creative farmers are using hard plastic molds that fit around the stem of a budding fruit or vegetable to grow produce in strange shapes: star-shaped cucumbers, square watermelons, and even these adorable "baby" pears. The fun fruit has become so popular that even some U.S. farmers are giving it a try.

CHEF OF THE FUTURE

WHO IBM'S WATSON (YES, THE SUPERCOMPUTER THAT WON ON *JEOPARDY!*)

WHAT WOWED HUNGRY CROWDS WITH ITS CULINARY CREATIONS

WHEN FEBRUARY 2014

WHERE AT THE IBM PULSE CONFERENCE IN LAS VEGAS, NEVADA, U.S.A.

HOW APPARENTLY WINNING ON *JEOPARDY!* WASN'T ENOUGH

FOR THIS SUPERCOMPUTER. WATSON'S BIG "BRAIN"—WHICH HAS STORED SOME 35,000 RECIPES—GAVE REAL-LIFE CHEFS ON THE TRUCK INFO TO PUT TOGETHER ODD (THOUGH SUPPOSEDLY DELICIOUS) DISHES. CHOCOLATE BURRITOS? KENYAN BRUSSELS SPROUTS? THERE'S NOW A COOKBOOK SO YOU CAN TRY WATSON'S INNOVATIVE CREATIONS FOR YOURSELF!

Now Serving

IBM.COM/COGNITIVECOOKING

NEWS FEED

>>> COPENHAGEN, DENMARK: IN A VIRAL VIDEO, THE DANISH NATIONAL CHAMBER ORCHESTRA GAVE A SIZZLING TANGO PERFORMANCE WHILE

MYSTERY SODA MACHINE KEEPS CUSTOMERS *GUESSING*

SEATTLE, WASHINGTON, U.S.A.

Calling all sleuths! Seattle has a spooky mystery to solve: Who is responsible for stocking the sodas in this old-school—some say haunted!—vending machine? No one knows exactly how the cans get into the machine, or who collects the 75 cents each one costs, even though it has been going on for years. Just press the "mystery" button, and await your sugary surprise.

FOOD *OR* FASHION?

NEW YORK, NEW YORK, U.S.A.

When actress India Menuez showed up at a dinner for French fashion label Chanel, all eyes were on her purse: a very realistic-looking bagel (sesame seeds and cream cheese included)—with a cross-body strap. Fashion blogs thought Chanel made the couture confection, but the plastic bagel bag was actually created by a Canadian artist whose other designs include bags shaped like baguettes, challah bread, and croissants.

EATING SUPER-SPICY CHILIES. SOME PERFORMERS LOOKED UNCOMFORTABLE—BUT AS THEY SAY, THE SHOW MUST GO ON.

SKY-HIGH DINING

TAKING FINE DINING TO NEW HEIGHTS!

THE NETHERLANDS

Are you afraid of heights? Then you may want to pass on dinner at CuliAir Sky Dining. The Dutch company offers hungry thrill seekers the chance to have a meal made and eaten aboard a hot air balloon! A professional chef prepares the food while hovering hundreds of feet in the air, even using the balloon's flame to cook parts of the dishes. The trip lasts about an hour and a half—dessert is served on solid ground after landing. But an experience like this doesn't come cheap: You'll pay 415 euros (about U.S. $460) for a dinner flight. CuliAir insists it's not as scary as it sounds, even if you're normally intimidated by tall places!

THREE COURSES ARE SERVED WHILE IN FLIGHT.

THE HOT-AIR BALLOON CAN HOLD 14 DINERS.

THE CULIAIR BALLOON FLIES HIGH OVER THE DUTCH COUNTRYSIDE, GIVING GUESTS A MEAL TO REMEMBER!

LIFESTYLES OF THE RICH 'N' HUNGRY

HAUTE DIGGITY DOG

SEATTLE, WASHINGTON, U.S.A.

The classic American hot dog got a fancy makeover in 2014, when Seattle food truck Tokyo Dog decided to best the reigning world record holder for the most expensive hot dog. The result: A foot-long (30.5-cm) smoked cheese bratwurst piled high with grilled onions, maitake mushrooms, black truffles, Wagyu beef, paddle-fish caviar, foie gras, and Japanese mayo. But paying more money for food doesn't always mean it tastes better. Local food writer Allecia Vermillion paid $169 to eat one. She says, "I liked the hot dog better by itself. All the fancy stuff on top made it taste kind of gross."

ALSO ON **THE MENU** AT **TOKYO DOG**: **FRIES** TOPPED WITH **SEAWEED!**

NEWS FEED

>>> FLORIDA, U.S.A.: IN OCTOBER 2014, ONE STARBUCKS CUSTOMER BEAT THE RECORD FOR THE MOST EXPENSIVE DRINK—A VANILLA LATTE WITH

TASTES EXPENSIVE

THE WORLD'S
TALLEST
STACK
OF PANCAKES
STOOD
2 FEET,
11 INCHES TALL
(91 CM)
AND WAS
MADE UP OF
242
PANCAKES!

PRICEY PANCAKES

MANCHESTER, ENGLAND

Would you pay $1,200 for a stack of pancakes? Big spenders had the opportunity to do just that at the Radisson Blu Edwardian's Opus One Bar and Restaurant on Pancake Day 2014. The chef whipped up a short stack wedge that contained some pricey seafood, plus Russian caviar, truffles, and a dollop of house-made hollandaise made from expensive champagne. That's a high price to pay when most people would rather have maple syrup!

THE WORLD'S MOST EXPENSIVE DOUGHNUT—
WHICH INCLUDES CHAMPAGNE JELLY AND EDIBLE DIAMONDS—
RECENTLY SOLD FOR $1,681.

THAT'S ONE GOLDEN SCOOP!

DUBAI, UNITED ARAB EMIRATES

Though technically not the world's most expensive dessert—that honor goes to a $25,000 sundae in New York City—the Black Diamond ice cream at Scoopi Café in Dubai sure costs a lot more than the sweet treats sold out of the noisy truck trolling your neighborhood. For 3,000 dirham (about U.S. $815) you get a single scoop of vanilla ice cream topped with rare saffron, black truffles, and teensy flakes of gold that you can actually eat. You'll want to eat slowly enough to savor your scoop, but not too slowly or you'll be left with an expensive melted mess!

101 ESPRESSO SHOTS THAT WOULD HAVE COST $83.75 IF HE HADN'T USED A COUPON FOR A FREE DRINK!

SAY WHAT?

THERE'S A SQUIRREL IN MY SOUP!

1881

For the most part, it seems the country's 20th president, James Garfield, had pretty normal tastes: He liked fresh bread, milk, and a kind of apple dessert called Garfield pie. But one of his favorite foods was squirrel soup! *The Original White House Cook Book,* published in 1887, says the soup is particularly delicious if you add "corn, Irish potatoes, tomatoes and Lima beans," but warns that you'll want to strain it first to get rid of those pesky squirrel bones.

PRESIDENT **RONALD REAGAN** KEPT **ACORNS** IN HIS **DESK DRAWER** TO **FEED** THE **SQUIRRELS** OUTSIDE THE **WHITE HOUSE.**

>>> U.S. PRESIDENTS' ECCENTRIC EATING HABITS

1923

VASELINE... WITH BREAKFAST?

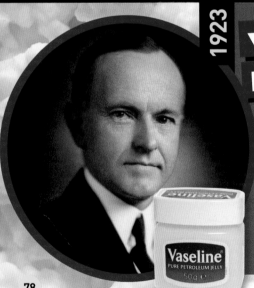

Who could make eating boring old boiled wheat and rye for breakfast even weirder? The 30th president of the United States, that's who. Calvin Coolidge preferred spooning down his favorite breakfast while having someone rub Vaseline on his head. Rumor has it that a servant had to do the unfortunate job.

Vaseline
PURE PETROLEUM JELLY
50g ℮

"I DO NOT LIKE BROCCOLI!"

PASS THE COTTAGE CHEESE, PLEASE!

Richard Nixon is known for being the only U.S. president who resigned from office. But a little fun fact that few know is that, like Coolidge, he had a weird breakfast habit: One of his favorite morning meals was cottage cheese ... topped with ketchup! He also ate yogurt, which he had flown in to the White House from California.

1969

EAT YOUR VEGGIES, GEORGE!

Do you hate broccoli? George H. W. Bush does. He hates it so much that during a speech he once said, "I do not like broccoli. I haven't liked it since I was a little kid and my mother made me eat it." But he didn't stop there, proclaiming, "I'm president of the United States, and I'm not going to eat any more broccoli." That's one unique use of a presidential veto!

1989

ENOUGH **JELLY BELLY BEANS** WERE EATEN IN 2014 TO CIRCLE THE **EARTH** MORE THAN FIVE TIMES.

1981

REAGAN LOVES JELLY BELLY

When you're the president, you get to do what you want. Ronald Reagan loved Jelly Belly jelly beans so much that for his inauguration, they supplied more than three tons (3.3 MT) of the sugary treat. Jelly Belly even created the blueberry flavor specifically for the event so there would be red, white, and blue! The 40th U.S. president also kept a giant jar of the beans on his desk in the Oval Office and on Air Force One.

A MOVABLE FEAST

WEIRD FEATS AND GOOD DEEDS

PUSHING STUART KETTELL
MOUNT A DART
MOUNT RUSSELL
WITH HIS SNOWD SPROUT
WITH HIS NO DO...

WE ARE MACMILLAN.
CANCER SUPPORT

WWW.WI... JULY 30th

A **SERVING** OF
BRUSSELS SPROUTS
CONTAINS MORE
VITAMIN C
THAN AN
ORANGE.

KETTELL
WORE THROUGH
22 BRUSSELS
SPROUTS
DURING HIS
CHALLENGE.

MOUNT SNOWDON, WALES

Some people just give money to charity, but what fun is that? Instead, Stuart Kettell comes up with crazy challenges to complete so people will donate big bucks to an organization that raises funds for cancer research.

Kettell's weirdest challenge so far (he's done ten as of 2015) happened in 2014, when he decided to push a Brussels sprout up Mount Snowdon—using his nose! Climbing the mountain itself is a challenge, but Kettell says that every year he has to come up with something different and even crazier than his past challenges. It took him four days of crawling and head bobbing to get the sprout 3,560 feet (1,085 m) to the top. Don't worry: He wore a special mask to protect his nose from all that action. "The most difficult part was the pain in my knees," Kettell says. "Even though I had knee pads. Also, the weather was terrible the last two days!"

The surprising stunt raised £7,500 (more than U.S. $11,500) for cancer research.

JUST HANGING AROUND: IN 2012, KETTELL SPENT AN ENTIRE WEEK HANGING BY HELIUM BALLOONS FOR SEVERAL HOURS A DAY INSIDE HIS FAVORITE SHOPPING MALL!

HOP TO IT!: IN 2015, KETTELL HOPPED ON A POGO STICK FOR SEVERAL DAYS TO POP 10,000 BALLOONS.

TERRIFYING TREAT

ALIEN ENCOUNTER

[CREEPY CAKES]

Would you readily bite into a dessert that looks as if it could bite you back? These creepy cakes are almost too spooky to eat!

HAPPY 8TH BIRTHDAY SETH!

SCORPION SURPRISE

IN ENGLAND,
"FLIES GRAVEYARD"
IS A **PASTRY** FILLED WITH
MINCEMEAT
(A JAM MADE WITH **SPICED DRIED FRUIT**).

DEADLY DELICIOUS

WOODSY WITCH

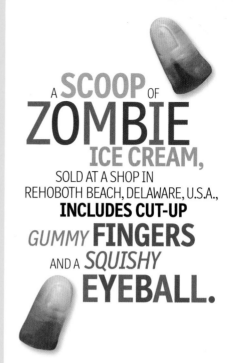

A **SCOOP** OF **ZOMBIE** **ICE CREAM,** SOLD AT A SHOP IN REHOBOTH BEACH, DELAWARE, U.S.A., **INCLUDES CUT-UP** *GUMMY* **FINGERS** AND A *SQUISHY* **EYEBALL.**

BAD TO THE BONE

MMMM … MAGGOTS!

BUG
BUFFET

CRICKET POWER!

PROTEIN-PACKED
CRICKET
BARS

CRICKET POWER
HAS NEARLY
TWiCE
AS MUCH **PROTEIN** AS
BEEF JERKY.

NEW YORK, NEW YORK, U.S.A.

If the thought of putting a noisy, hopping cricket into your mouth makes you go *"Ewwwwww,"* you're not alone. But that didn't stop Exo co-founders Greg Sewitz and Gabi Lewis, who were looking to create a snack that was both healthy and delicious. In 2013, the college roommates ordered a box of 2,000 crickets, then froze them, roasted them, and blended them into a fine powder. They used the protein-rich flour to make bars that were not only good for you but tasty as well. Thanks to the bars' surprising popularity, Exo now makes four different flavors—each containing about 40 crickets!

NEWS FEED

>>> NICE, FRANCE: A FRENCH CHEF SAYS MICHELIN (A COMPANY THAT AWARDS STARS TO THE WORLD'S BEST RESTAURANTS) TOOK AWAY HIS STAR IN 2014

BAMBOO WORMS, BEETLES, AND CRICKETS, OH ... YUM?

BANGKOK, THAILAND

Walk through any outdoor food market in Thailand and you'll likely spot heaps of fried insects that are seasoned and ready for snacking. Students at professional cooking school Le Cordon Bleu's Bangkok branch got a lesson in local eating in 2015 during a special seminar on the tastiness and nutritional value of creepy crawlers. Cricket soup, giant beetle crisps, and bamboo worm desserts were just some of the outrageous offerings on the menu. This may be the only time bugs were actually invited into the school's kitchen.

AT **STREET MARKETS** IN **BANGKOK,** YOU CAN **SAMPLE FRIED SCORPIONS, CENTIPEDES,** AND **LOCUSTS.**

80 PERCENT OF THE WORLD EATS INSECTS REGULARLY.

WHO'S HUNGRY?

RALEIGH, NORTH CAROLINA, U.S.A.

At the North Carolina Museum of Natural Sciences, insects aren't just kept in glass boxes on display. Every fall, the museum hosts BugFest, a celebration of all things buggy that draws more than 35,000 people from miles around. A fan favorite is Café Insecta, where local chefs cook up crickets, mealworms, and more to give daring diners a chance to try something they wouldn't normally get to eat. Bug snacks not for you? The free festival also includes live music, movies, educational talks, and plenty of hands-on activities.

BECAUSE HE STARTED SERVING INSECTS. A MICHELIN SPOKES-PERSON DISAGREES—BUT THE CHEF IS STILL STEAMED.

TRAIL OF
TACOS

GUADALAJARA, MEXICO

IN FEBRUARY 2015, IT TOOK 130 PEOPLE SIX HOURS AND MORE THAN A TON (0.9 MT) OF PORK TO CREATE THIS EPIC LINE OF TACOS, which stretched for nearly two miles (3.2 km)! The tacos were the kind you'd typically find as street food in Mexico, made with small corn tortillas, seasoned meat (they used a regional specialty called *cochinita pibil*), and onions. The crazy project—which was an attempt to break the world record for the longest line of tacos—took place at a huge festival set up to entice tourists to visit Mexico. Lucky bystanders also benefited—free tacos!

PICKY EATER OR SUPER-TASTER?

Have you ever been called a picky eater? Fear not! You may just be a supertaster: someone with a sense of taste so great that they experience the five basic tastes—sweet, salty, sour, umami (savory), and bitter—with more intensity than the average person.

Find out if there's a scientific reason for not liking grapefruit, coffee, and broccoli by taking this simple test (with a grown-up around, please!).

THANKS TO THEIR **GENETIC MAKEUP,** SOME PEOPLE THINK **CILANTRO** TASTES LIKE **SOAP!**

SUPERTASTER *TASTE TEST*

WHAT YOU'LL NEED:

- BOTTLE OF FOOD COLORING
  (DARK COLORS WORK BEST)
- COTTON SWABS
- HOLE PUNCH REINFORCEMENTS
- MAGNIFYING GLASS

DIRECTIONS:

FIRST, USING A COTTON SWAB, APPLY THE FOOD COLORING TO COAT THE FRONT PART OF YOUR TONGUE. YOU'LL PROBABLY NEED TO USE A MIRROR. NOTICE HOW THE DYE STAINS YOUR TONGUE BUT SLIDES OFF THOSE LITTLE PINK BUMPS CALLED PAPILLAE, WHICH HOLD THE TASTE BUDS.

NEXT, TAKE ONE OF THE HOLE PUNCH REINFORCEMENTS AND PLACE IT ON THE DYED AREA OF YOUR TONGUE. HOLDING YOUR TONGUE VERY STILL SO THE PAPER REINFORCEMENT DOESN'T MOVE, ASK A GROWN-UP TO COUNT HOW MANY OF THE PINK PAPILLAE THEY SEE INSIDE THE RING. THIS IS WHERE YOU'LL NEED THAT MAGNIFYING GLASS.

HOW MANY DID YOU FIND?

Supertasters will have more than 35 papillae, and average tasters will have somewhere between 15 and 35. If you found fewer than 15, you're known as a non-taster, meaning your taste buds require a little more pep—like super spicy or bitter flavors—to please!

CHAPTER 5

STRANGE
SCIENCE

ALIVE! • ALIEN OF THE AMAZON • THIS FROG HAS
SES NUCLEAR MISHAP • ARGH! TEEN FOILS PIRAT
AIGHT TO THE HEART • ROCKETING TOWARD SAFER
• PART HUMAN, PART MACHINE • C
CROCS AT PLAY

KERMIT'S LONG-LOST COUSIN, PAGE 94

MUSHROOM LOOKS LIKE FUN GUY

HI-HO, HI-HO!

NORFOLK, ENGLAND

A newly identified species of mushroom can look like a tiny person. The mushroom, which turns out to be common along roadsides, had previously been identified as a variant of another, very rare species of mushroom. But DNA analysis found it to be a species of its own, complete with "arms" and a sizable head topped by a little cap. Now people keep their eyes peeled to spot the fungus among us.

ARGH! TEEN FOILS PIRATE PLOT

WHO NINTH-GRADE STUDENT HADAIA AZAD EZZULDDIN

WHAT CREATED AN EASY, INEXPENSIVE WAY TO PREVENT PEOPLE FROM PIRATING (ILLEGALLY RECORDING) MOVIES BY PLACING INFRARED LIGHTS BEHIND A MOVIE SCREEN. THE LIGHTS CAN'T BE SEEN BY PEOPLE WATCHING THE MOVIE, BUT THEY DISTORT THE IMAGES RECORDED BY CAMERAS.

WHERE ERBIL, IRAQ

WHY MOVIE PIRACY IS A HUGE PROBLEM THAT TAKES MONEY FROM THOUSANDS OF PEOPLE. INSTALLING INFRARED BEAMS IS EASIER THAN MAKING PERPETRATORS WALK THE PLANK.

NEWS FEED

>>> HULL, ENGLAND: A SCIENTIST CALCULATED THAT SPIDER-MAN WOULD NEED TO EAT A 900-EGG OMELET TO MAKE ENOUGH SILK TO SWING

EXCUSE ME, PLEASE!

DEEP SPACE

Scientists watched a black hole gobble up a sun-size star—well, almost all of it! It was once believed that the tug of a black hole was so strong nothing could escape its pull. But astronomers suspected that mysterious jets of light in outer space might actually be cosmic "burps" from black holes as they struggled to swallow large, gassy meals. At long last, a black hole was polite enough to provide the evidence.

KITTY LITTER
CAUSES
NUCLEAR MISHAP

CAUTION

RADIATION AREA

RWP REQUIRED FOR ENTRY

OUTSIDE CARLSBAD, NEW MEXICO, U.S.A.

Kitty litter was behind a radiation leak at a facility used to store nuclear waste. The leak happened after someone used "organic" kitty litter instead of the old-fashioned kind, which contains clay that absorbs radioactive waste. The new litter, which did not contain clay, was unable to prevent the radiation release. Luckily no one was hurt, but the plant has been shut down until it can be made safe again.

ME-OW!

THROUGH A SINGLE SCENE OF THE MOVIE. THE PROTEIN-RICH MEAL WOULD LET THE WEB-SLINGER SPIN SILK AS STRONG AS PIANO WIRE.

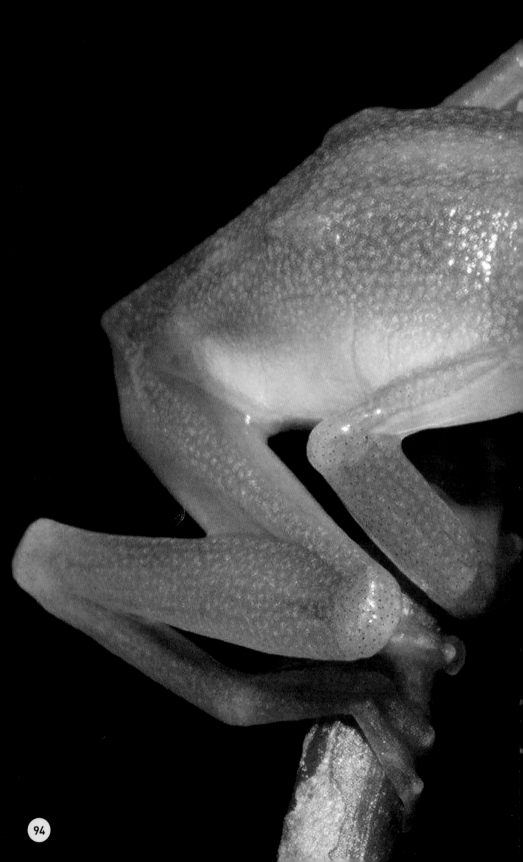

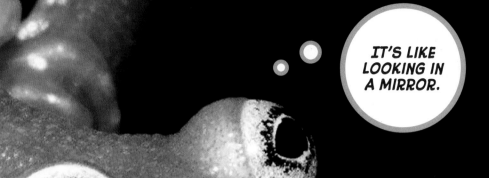

IT'S LIKE LOOKING IN A MIRROR.

KERMiT'S

LONG-LOST COUSiN

TALAMANCA MOUNTAINS, COSTA RICA

KERMIT THE FROG SAYS IT'S NOT EASY BEING GREEN, BUT THE COLOR SURE HELPS WHEN YOU'RE HANGING OUT IN THE RAIN FOREST. This small frog, which resembles the well-known Muppet, surprised scientists, who thought most frog species in the Costa Rican rain forest had already been discovered. The big-eyed amphibians, which scientists named *Hyalinobatrachium dianae*, had gone unnoticed not only because they blend in with their environment, but also because the frogs tend to hang out on the underside of leaves. Top that off with an unusual insectlike call, and it's no surprise it hopped under the radar for so long.

FREAKY
ANIMAL FINDS

IT'S ALIVE!

SEA SQUIRTS
MIGHT LOOK LIKE
BLOBS,
BUT THEY HAVE
SPINAL CORDS.

COASTLINE OF CHILE AND PERU

It may not walk and talk, but this "rock" is alive and well. The unusual animal is actually a type of sea squirt—sacklike creatures that spend their lives sitting on the ocean floor. Sea squirts draw water into their bodies through one of two openings, filter out tiny bits of food, then squirt the water out the exit hole. Because the animals can't move once they settle, their rocky outer covering likely provides a bit of protection from predators. But it doesn't fool the local people, who happily munch them for lunch.

NEWS FEED

>>> SAKHA REPUBLIC, RUSSIA: IN 2015, A RUSSIAN HUNTER FOUND A PATCH OF HAIR STUCK IN FROZEN GROUND . IT TURNED OUT TO BE THE REMAINS OF A

ONE SPECIES OF

SLIME-MOLD BEETLE
CALLED *A. VADERI* IS NAMED AFTER *STAR WARS* VILLAIN

DARTH VADER.

ALIEN OF THE AMAZON

GURUPI RIVER, BRAZIL

A big-eyed catfish snagged a name from *Star Wars* when the scientist who discovered it realized it looked a bit like one of the movie's characters. *Peckoltia greedoi* is named after Greedo, an alien defeated by Han Solo in *Episode IV*. Researchers assign names to newly discovered species to make it easier to discuss the critters with other scientists. Let's hope this one fares better than its namesake!

FANGED FROGS USE THEIR *BONY* "FANGS" WHEN FIGHTING ONE ANOTHER.

THIS FROG HAS FANGS!

SULAWESI, INDONESIA

A newly discovered species of frog isn't fascinating because of its fangs, but because females give birth to live tadpoles. It's the only frog known to do so; most frogs lay eggs in water, although a few carry their eggs in special pouches to keep them safe. But the fanged frogs surprised scientists. One even gave birth in a scientist's hand!

BABY WOOLLY RHINO—THE ONLY COMPLETE YOUNGSTER OF THE SPECIES (WHICH WENT EXTINCT ABOUT 10,000 YEARS AGO) ANYONE HAS EVER FOUND.

CRATERS
PLAGUE THE

YAMAL PENINSULA, SIBERIA, RUSSIA

A SERIES OF DEEP CRATERS HAVE BEEN SPOTTED IN AN AREA OF SIBERIA SO FROZEN AND REMOTE IT'S NICKNAMED "END OF THE WORLD." Most craters are made by meteors from outer space slamming into the Earth, but scientists believe the cause in this case is coming from *inside* the Earth. The area, which has been frozen in a thick layer of permafrost, has begun to thaw. The loss of ice releases methane, an explosive gas, into pockets trapped under the ground. The theory is the growing pressure eventually causes the surface to explode outward, creating a gaping hole in the Earth.

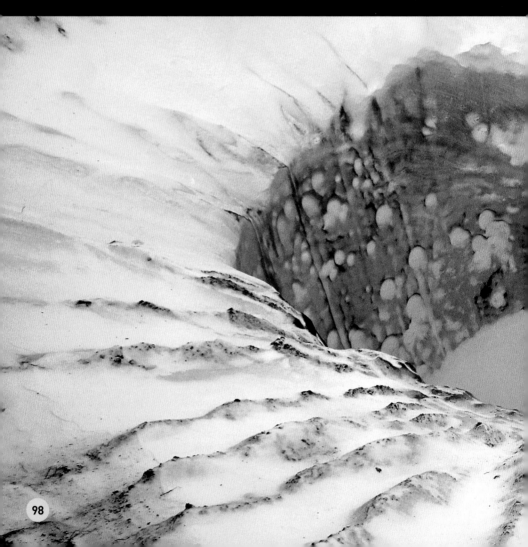

END *OF THE* WORLD

MOST PEOPLE *CAN'T LICK* THEIR OWN **ELBOW.** TRY IT!

REMOTE-CONTROL BULLFIGHTING

STRAIGHT TO THE HEART

1929

Searching for a way to get medicine directly into the heart, physician Werner Forssmann decided to test one possible method—on himself. He numbed his elbow and then inserted a narrow tube into a vein in his arm. After pushing more than two feet (65 cm) of the tube into the vein, Forssmann walked down the hospital hall to the x-ray room, where a quick image proved he had reached his target.

1965

José Delgado found that small zaps of electricity to the brain could change an animal's behavior. The scientist demonstrated his discovery by facing down a charging bull. A remote control in his hand allowed Delgado to stop the bull with a press of a button, which stimulated electrodes implanted in the bull's brain. The experiment eventually led to treatment for people with certain types of brain disorders.

>>> SCIENTISTS GO TO GREAT LENGTHS

1954

ROCKETING TOWARD SAFER EVACUATIONS

U.S. Air Force pilots sometimes have to eject from their planes at high speeds. Wanting to ensure the safety of such events, Colonel John Paul Stapp put his own body to the test. He strapped himself to a rocket sled that raced along a track at 632 miles an hour (1,017 km/h) and then stopped in just 1.4 seconds. The sudden stop made Stapp go temporarily blind, but he proved that—if necessary—humans could safely eject from their planes at such a high speed.

PART HUMAN, PART MACHINE

1998

Kevin Warwick wanted to be more than human, so he turned himself into a cyborg. A radio device temporarily placed in his arm let him open doors and turn on lights without lifting a finger. He later had electrodes implanted in nerves in his arm. The electrodes allowed him to move a wheelchair and artificial hand without touching them.

1984

MMMM ... BACTERIA SOUP!

> A TEASPOON OF **SOIL** CONTAINS AS MANY AS **ONE BILLION BACTERIA.**

After treating patients with stomach ulcers, Barry Marshall discovered the bleeding sores were caused by bacteria called *H. pylori.* Other doctors scoffed when Marshall shared his news, insisting ulcers were caused by stress. So the confident physician drank a broth containing the bacteria and gave himself an ulcer, proving he was right. A quick dose of antibiotic cleared up the infection, and Marshall was awarded the Nobel Prize.

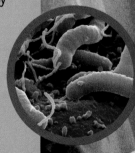

101

VAN GOGH'S
EAR ON TOUR

BLEND OF ART AND SCIENCE BRINGS FAMOUS BODY PART TO LIFE

BOSTON, MASSACHUSETTS, U.S.A.

Vincent van Gogh's severed ear may be part of his claim to fame, but artist Diemut Strebe decided to create a living replica of the complete body part using cells from one of van Gogh's relatives. Strebe collected cartilage cells from the ear of van Gogh's great-great-grandnephew, who carries one-sixteenth of his famous relative's DNA. Scientists then grew the cells in a nutrient-rich solution. Strebe re-created the missing ear with a computer-imaging program, and then scientists used 3-D printing to construct the ear from the new cells. The result is a ghostly, floating ear kept alive in its watery showcase. What's even weirder, the ear "listens" when people speak. A computer converts spoken words into signals that mimic nerve pulses, just as the nerves of the ear send sound signals to the brain. Speakers attached to the computer system play crackling sounds similar to those made when nerves are recorded, allowing visitors to experience the ear from the inside and out.

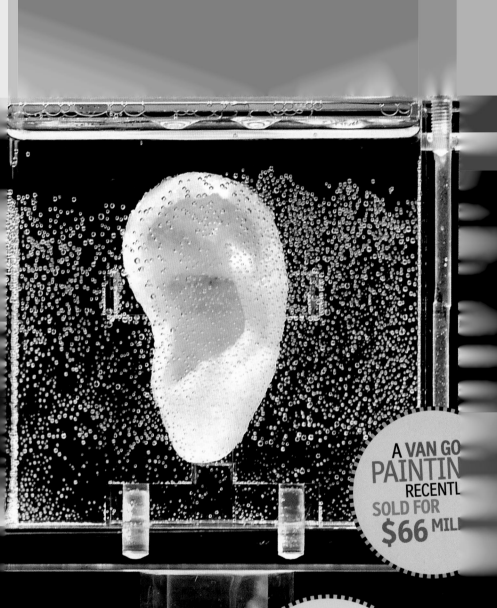

A VAN GO[GH]
PAINTIN[G]
RECENTL[Y]
SOLD FOR
$66 MIL[LION]

VAN GOGH
SAID HE *CUT OFF*
A PIECE OF
HIS OWN EARLOBE
AFTER **A FIGHT**
WITH A FRIEND,
ARTIST
PAUL GAUGUIN.

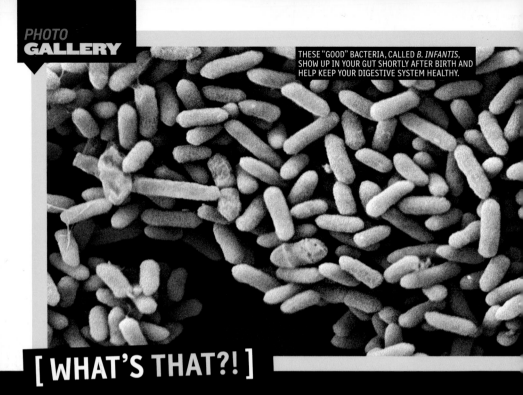

THESE "GOOD" BACTERIA, CALLED *B. INFANTIS*, SHOW UP IN YOUR GUT SHORTLY AFTER BIRTH AND HELP KEEP YOUR DIGESTIVE SYSTEM HEALTHY.

[WHAT'S THAT?!]

Think you're all alone? Think again. Your body is crawling with all kinds of itty-bitty critters and other microscopic marvels. Check out these creepy houseguests.

SOME **MiCROBES** USE **NATURAL OiLS** ON **YOUR BODY** AS **FOOD.**

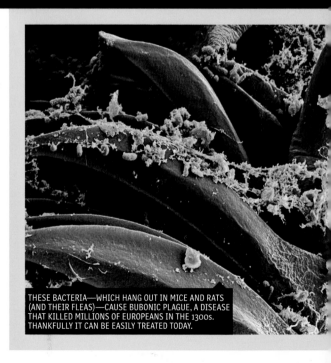

THESE BACTERIA—WHICH HANG OUT IN MICE AND RATS (AND THEIR FLEAS)—CAUSE BUBONIC PLAGUE, A DISEASE THAT KILLED MILLIONS OF EUROPEANS IN THE 1300s. THANKFULLY IT CAN BE EASILY TREATED TODAY.

THOSE PINK THINGS BURIED AT THE BASE OF THESE EYELASHES? THEY'RE EYELASH MITES. AND EVERYBODY'S GOT 'EM.

MICROBE CELLS LIVING **IN** AND **ON YOU** OUTNUMBER YOUR OWN CELLS BY ABOUT **10** TO **1.**

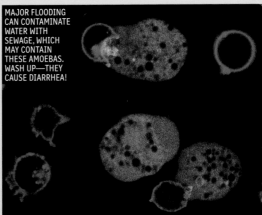

MAJOR FLOODING CAN CONTAMINATE WATER WITH SEWAGE, WHICH MAY CONTAIN THESE AMOEBAS. WASH UP—THEY CAUSE DIARRHEA!

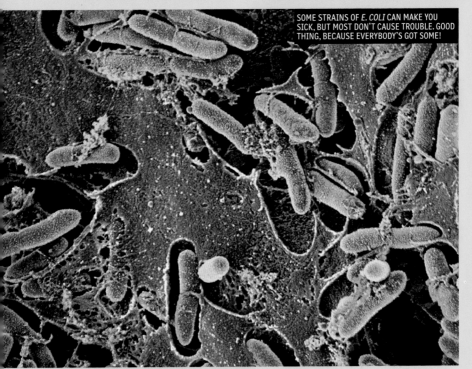

SOME STRAINS OF *E. COLI* CAN MAKE YOU SICK, BUT MOST DON'T CAUSE TROUBLE. GOOD THING, BECAUSE EVERYBODY'S GOT SOME!

A SHAVE A DAY KEEPS THE MOTHS AWAY

NANTOU COUNTY, TAIWAN

To find out whether the white "mustache" on the face of the brown huntsman spider helps the eight-legged predators find food, scientists shaved the white hairs from the faces of some spiders, while leaving others in place. After hundreds of hours spent watching the two groups hunt, they learned the spiders' mustaches lure mothy meals.

OCTOPUS CAUSES INTERNET FRENZY

WHO OCTOPUS AT MIDDLEBURY COLLEGE

WHAT GRABBED A CAMERA LEFT BY A FILMMAKER AND A SCIENTIST AND TURNED IT ON THE DUO, SNAPPING PHOTOS OF THE UNSUSPECTING PAIR

WHERE MIDDLEBURY, VERMONT, U.S.A.

WHY OBSERVERS SAY THE OCTOPUS TRIED TO EAT THE CAMERA AFTER SNAPPING THE STILLS, SO IT MAY SIMPLY HAVE BEEN SEARCHING FOR A SNACK.

OUTCOME A PHOTO OF THE SURPRISED FILMMAKER MADE THE ROUNDS ON THE INTERNET, GETTING A WHOPPING TWO MILLION VIEWS IN JUST ONE DAY.

NEWS FEED

>>> LONDON, ENGLAND: SCIENTISTS RECENTLY CREATED THE WORLD'S DARKEST MATERIAL. CALLED VANTABLACK, IT TRAPS ALMOST ALL INCOMING LIGHT SO IT

CAUTION: CROCS AT PLAY

KNOXVILLE, TENNESSEE, U.S.A.

It turns out alligators and crocodiles are more than just toothy predators—they're a surprisingly playful bunch. A researcher from University of Tennessee found the cold-blooded crocodilians surfing swells, snapping at streams of water, and tossing toys in their enclosures. The rough-and-tumble reptiles even rode piggyback on their pals.

STUNNING SCIENCE

HEFEI, ANHUI PROVINCE, CHINA

Scientists used ultra-high definition video to capture the beauty of chemical reactions. Dancing droplets, swirling smoke, burbling bubbles, and climbing crystals came to life as part of the Beautiful Chemistry project, which zoomed deep into the test tube to take viewers to the heart of each chemical reaction. Who knew science could be so beautiful?

DOESN'T REFLECT ONTO LENSES IN SPACE. ON EARTH, IT APPEARS TO TURN ANYTHING IT TOUCHES INTO A BLACK HOLE.

THE FUN SIDE OF SCIENCE

Science doesn't have to be serious all the time. Even fun experiments can make major scientific contributions. Guess what serious science these fun studies represent. Answers are at the bottom of the page.

1.

Scientists determined that it takes 2,500 licks to get to the center of a lollipop. The scientists were trying to figure out:

A. THE IDEAL SIZE FOR A NEW LINE OF LOLLIPOPS.

B. HOW WATER ERODES SOMETHING SOLID.

C. HOW LONG THE PAPER STICK CAN STAND UP TO SALIVA.

2.

Researchers zoomed remote-control planes (called drones) over a wildlife park in India where rhinos tend to hang out. The researchers did this because they want to:

A. STOP POACHERS FROM KILLING THE RHINOS.

B. SEE IF RHINOS PAY ATTENTION TO BIRDLIKE OBJECTS.

C. HERD THE RHINOS INTO ANOTHER AREA OF THE PARK.

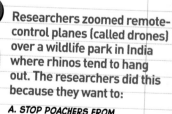
RHINOS HAVE ONLY **ONE** PREDATOR— US.

3. Scientists studied cats in boxes to see:

A. IF THEY SLEEP LONGER IN TOTAL DARKNESS.

B. WHETHER BOXES HELP CATS KEEP CALM.

C. IF THEY COULD RECOGNIZE THEIR OWNERS' VOICES.

HUBBLE CONFIRMED THAT THE **UNIVERSE** IS EXPANDING.

What did the Hubble telescope spot in space?

A. IDENTICAL EXPLODING STARS

B. THE CENTER OF THE UNIVERSE

C. LIGHT DISTORTED BY THE SUPERSTRONG GRAVITATIONAL PULL OF DISTANT GALAXIES

4.

TROPICAL STORMS TEND TO HAVE **MORE RAINFALL** THAN FULL-BLOWN HURRICANES.

5. This umbrella is:

A. THE NEWEST WAY TO MEASURE RAINFALL.

B. A TOP SECRET LISTENING DEVICE.

C. RIGGED SO IT WON'T BLOW INSIDE OUT.

CHAPTER 6

WAY-OUT TRAVEL

MORE LOVE LOCKS! · DUMPSTER DIVER EATS
MAN CRUISES THROUGH LIFE ON FANCY BOAT
R HEAD, YOUNG JEDI · BIZARRE BOARDING · R
OND? · NUCLEAR-POWERED SPACE TRAVEL ·
NUCLEAR-POWERED SPACE TRAVEL · NASA
GRACE DOUGHNUT · POPPI

LAIR OF THE LIZARD KING,
PAGE 115

NO MORE LOVE LOCKS!

PARIS, FRANCE

For years, couples in love have been attaching padlocks to the Pont des Arts bridge in Paris, then throwing the key into the river below to signify their unbreakable bond. But the bulky locks became too heavy for the bridge to support, causing parts of it to collapse—so officials decided to cut the locks loose! There's no word on whether it affected the lovebirds.

WOMAN CRUISES THROUGH LIFE ON FANCY BOAT

WHO EIGHTY-SIX-YEAR-OLD "MAMA LEE" WACHTSTETTER

WHAT SHE SPENDS $164,000 A YEAR TO LIVE ABOARD THE SWANKY CRUISE SHIP *CRYSTAL SERENITY.*

WHERE THE WORLD'S SEAS

WHY FOR THE LAST SEVEN YEARS, WACHTSTETTER HAS CHOSEN TO LIVE AT SEA—

A LIFESTYLE SHE TOOK UP AFTER HER HUSBAND, WHO INTRODUCED HER TO CRUISING, PASSED AWAY. ABOARD THE BOAT SHE GETS TO EAT, SLEEP, DANCE, WATCH MOVIES, TRAVEL THE WORLD, AND GENERALLY LIVE LIKE A QUEEN!

NEWS FEED

>>> LÜDERITZ, NAMIBIA: AN AFRICAN TOWN CHANGED ITS NAME BACK TO ITS ORIGINAL NAME—!NAMI≠NÜS—USING PUNCTUATION TO REPRESENT

DUMPSTER DIVER *EATS HIS WAY* ACROSS EUROPE

WARSAW, POLAND

They say one man's trash is another man's treasure, but for Baptiste Dubanchet, one man's trash was lunch! The Frenchman wanted to demonstrate how much perfectly good food is thrown away, so he biked 1,900 miles (3,000 km) from Paris to Warsaw eating nothing but garbage from supermarkets and restaurants! Dubanchet said staying full on the ten-week trip was actually easier than he expected.

TRAVELING IN THE LAP OF LUXURY

ABU DHABI, UNITED ARAB EMIRATES

The flight from London to Abu Dhabi aboard Etihad Airways' Airbus A380 just got a whole lot "suite-er." In 2014, the airline started selling tickets for new three-room luxury suites. A $20,000 ticket books you into the Residence, the plane's swanki-est pad, complete with a private bathroom, personal butler, and in-flight chef. Talk about a pampered plane ride!

CLICKLIKE SOUNDS USED IN THE LOCAL LANGUAGE. BUT SOME FOLKS AREN'T HAPPY, SAYING THE NAME WILL BE HARD TO PRONOUNCE AND DETER TOURISTS.

BIG-SCREEN HOTEL THEMES

AN INN FIT FOR HOBBITS

DURBUY, BELGIUM

Attention, fans of *The Lord of the Rings:* There's a hotel in Belgium where the rooms look like they've been pulled from the pages of J. R. R. Tolkien's blockbuster books! There are ten very different rooms at La Balade des Gnomes, each featuring different quirky amenities like a wooden hot tub, a starlit "sky" ceiling, and troll-friendly beds that look like they've been carved straight from a tree. Hungry for more? Check out the owner's wacky restaurant, La Gargouille (the gargoyle), next door.

A **SIGNED FIRST-EDITION** COPY OF *THE HOBBIT* RECENTLY SOLD FOR MORE THAN **$200,000.**

NEWS FEED

>>> **LONDON, ENGLAND:** HARRY POTTER FANS CAN CHECK INTO THE NEW WIZARD CHAMBERS AT THE GEORGIAN HOUSE HOTEL. THE ROOMS—DECKED OUT IN

THERE HAVE BEEN **30** OFFICIAL GODZILLA MOVIES MADE.

LAIR OF THE LIZARD KING

TOKYO, JAPAN

For more than 60 years, the King of the Monsters has been storming through Tokyo's city streets, scaring everyone and everything in his path. Now he has his sights set on a single neighborhood: Tokyo's Shinjuku district. You can't miss the nearly 40-foot (12-m)-tall Godzilla head that looms above Hotel Gracery. Six of the rooms there look out onto the scary statue—imagine that face greeting you in the morning! Two rooms feature giant claws, human-size monster models, and other ghastly decorations. Let's hope giant reptiles don't give you nightmares.

THE *MAKE-BELIEVE* **PLANET** TATOOINE GOT ITS **NAME** FROM A TOWN IN **TUNISIA** CALLED TATAOUINE.

REST YOUR HEAD, YOUNG JEDI

MATMATA, TUNISIA

A long time ago in a galaxy far, far away, a famous movie was filmed at ... a quirky little hotel in northern Africa? Hôtel Sidi Driss has become known as the "*Star Wars* hotel" because it was used as the inside set for Luke Skywalker's childhood home on Tatooine. The set decorations used in the movies are still in place inside the building—which has been around for hundreds of years. You can even eat in the Skywalker family dining room. But don't expect glitz and glamour in a galaxy far away. The cavernous rooms lack windows, and many other creature comforts.

POTION BOTTLES, SPELL BOOKS, AND FOUR-POSTER BEDS—ARE PERFECT FOR MUGGLES WHO WANT TO FEEL LIKE THEY'RE HUNKERING DOWN AT HOGWARTS.

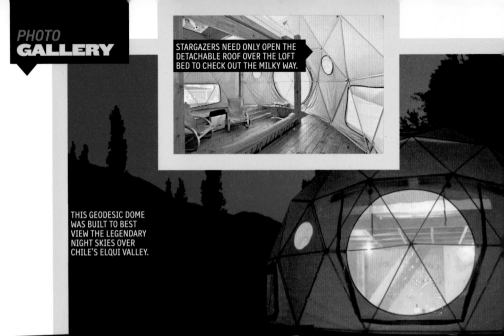

STARGAZERS NEED ONLY OPEN THE DETACHABLE ROOF OVER THE LOFT BED TO CHECK OUT THE MILKY WAY.

THIS GEODESIC DOME WAS BUILT TO BEST VIEW THE LEGENDARY NIGHT SKIES OVER CHILE'S ELQUI VALLEY.

[BIZARRE BOARDING]

Airbnb is a service that lets average folks rent out their homes—or domes— to vacationers. For a truly memorable overnight stay, skip the ho-hum hotels and book one of these weird lodges for your next family vacay!

YOU'LL FIND THE STANDARD BEDROOMS AND KITCHEN HERE, BUT THE COOLEST PART IS THIS TOP ROOM WITH 360-DEGREE VIEWS OF THE CITY!

IT'S HARD TO TELL UP FROM DOWN IN THIS THREE-LEVEL CUBEHOUSE LOCATED IN ROTTERDAM, THE NETHERLANDS.

MORE THAN
1,400 CASTLES
ARE LISTED ON THE
AIRBNB WEBSITE.

IN 2015, FRENCH SKI RESORT COURCHEVEL LISTED ONE OF ITS CABLE CARS ON AIRBNB AND GAVE ONE WINNER THE CHANCE TO SPEND THE NIGHT IN THE SKY.

THE CAR WAS TRANSFORMED INTO A SUITE FOR THE PROMOTION, INCLUDING A BEDROOM AND LIVING ROOM.

AIRBNB **CONTEST WINNERS** HAVE *STAYED THE NIGHT* AT **FENWAY PARK,** HOME OF THE **BOSTON RED SOX.**

IT'S JUST A COZY SPACE FOR TWO TO SLEEP INDOORS, BUT THERE ARE BATHROOM FACILITIES JUST NEXT DOOR.

LIVE LIKE A PIONEER IN THIS COLORFUL, WACKY WAGON POSITIONED NEAR THE SEA IN CORNWALL, ENGLAND.

DON'T LOOK DOWN!

UP, UP, AND AWAY!

ROCKIN' RETREAT

ROOM WITH A VIEW!

GRANDES AND PETITES JORASSES MOUNTAINS, ITALY

YOU CAN'T PULL THE CAR UP TO THIS SIMPLE ITALIAN CAMPSITE—you have to descend an ultrasteep rock face to get there. The solar-powered Bivouac Gervasutti is located more than 9,300 feet (2,835 m) above sea level, deep in the Italian Alps. It's designed as a secret hideaway of sorts for extreme adventurers who dare to make the descent. The cabin is equipped with a dining room and enough sleeping space for 12 travelers. The best part—besides the amazing views—it's only $10 per night... if

NO SELFIE STICKS HERE!

PHOTOGRAPHER SHARES UPSIDE-DOWN TRAVEL PICS

MOSCOW, RUSSIA

No tricks here—these are, indeed, photos of a man balancing on his head. Photographer Anton Charushin has become a social media sensation with his crazy cool travel photos featuring him doing split-second, hands-free headstands in picturesque places around the world. He has used this trick—which he learned break dancing in high school—to precariously perch on rock ledges, in grassy fields, on stairs, in pools, and near famous landmarks in more than a dozen countries.

Charushin looks so calm and perfectly still that you'd think the photos are fakes. And though he admits to occasionally using software filters to make the photos prettier, he insists that "the headstand is always original and all places are real." But he doesn't do it alone—he usually asks a friend to snap the pics while he's in position!

CHARUSHIN INVENTED THE WORD "STOLBYSHKING" TO DESCRIBE THE ACT OF STANDING ON ONE'S HEAD IN INTERESTING PLACES.

THE PHOTOGRAPHER'S FAVORITE PHOTO: HEAD-STANDING IN HALONG BAY, VIETNAM.

THIS PHOTO MIGHT LOOK LIKE IT WAS TAKEN IN CHINA, BUT IT WAS ACTUALLY TAKEN IN ETHNOMIR, A CULTURAL PROJECT IN RUSSIA.

NASA SCRAPS PLANS FOR PERMANENT MOON BASE

NUCLEAR-POWERED SPACE TRAVEL

1958

Scientists spent a lot of time developing Project Orion: a plan to use atomic bombs to propel a skyscraper-size spacecraft into the cosmos. But the obvious risk of radiation exposure to the astronauts on board and people standing near the takeoff site meant this idea never got off the ground.

After man set foot on the moon, scientists set their sites on building him a place to stay. In 1968, it was proposed that the Apollo moon missions land at the same site and leave behind large loads of materials to build a kind of home on the moon, which astronauts could use by 1980. But Congress cut NASA's funding, and the big budget for Moonbase Apollo was never approved.

1968

>>> **TO INFINITY ... AND BEYOND?**

1964

AN UNEXPECTED CONTENDER IN THE SPACE RACE

A Zambian schoolteacher claimed Africa would beat the United States and the Soviet Union in their race to conquer outer space using his plan for a rocket made of aluminum and copper. He planned to catapult a team of eleven Zambians, plus two cats, to Mars—a planet he claimed to have studied at a secret headquarters and said was filled with primitive natives. Unsurprisingly, he was never considered a serious contender to exit Earth's atmosphere.

THE **ASTRONAUTS** TRAINED BY *ROLLING DOWN A HILL* IN AN **OIL DRUM.**

THE *AVERAGE* TEMPERATURE ON VENUS IS 864°F (462°C).

NEXT STOP ...
VENUS!

2014

Although modern space exploration has mostly focused on Mars, a couple of scientists think we may want to head to Venus next instead. NASA researchers Dale Arney and Chris Jones say that although Mars is definitely more Earthlike—and Venus's blazing temperature much too hot for humans—they've come up with a plan to build a colony of airships that would hover in Venus's clouds 31 miles (50 km) above the planet's surface. For now, Project Genesis is strictly an idea, but who knows what the future will bring?

1975

STANFORD SUGGESTS EARTHLIKE SPACE DOUGHNUT

Imagine living in a doughnut-shaped space station with Earthlike gravity big enough to house 10,000 people. Nope, this isn't a sci-fi movie plot. It's the Stanford Torus, a design that NASA considered during a study of possible space habitats. Paintings of the living space make it look roomy and green—potentially a far cry from what real space colonies would be like.

ONE CRAZY DAY IN DUBAI

DUBAI, UNITED ARAB EMIRATES

Everything's larger than life in Dubai, home of the world's tallest building, largest man-made island, and biggest shopping mall by total area. Nicknamed the "City of Gold" for good reason, you won't want to miss these wild attractions:

VISIT:

The hottest ticket in town is the soon-to-open Museum of the Future. The coolest thing you'll find inside this silver space-age building? A research lab, where you can visit and watch people working on new inventions to shape the future.

PLAY:

For some freshwater fun, hop over to the Jumeirah Creekside hotel and take a dip in the eighth-floor swimming pool with a glass bottom overlooking the hotel lobby. Or if Dubai's sweltering heat has got you craving something even cooler, head to Ski Dubai and whiz through the air on the Snow Bullet, the world's first indoor subzero zip line! The side-by-side swing seats are perfect for racing a friend or family member 492 feet (150 m) through the air, which is set at a frigid 24.8°F (-4°C)!

EAT:

Once you've worked up an appetite from all the fun activities Dubai has to offer, you'll want to book a seat on the Boardwalk BBQ Donut, an inflatable ring outfitted for grilling while you float down Dubai Creek. If barbecue isn't your thing, don't worry—in Dubai you can find food from all over the world! Japanese sushi? They've got it. Lebanese shawarma? You bet. You can even find American cheeseburgers!

STAY:

Sleeping with the fishes takes on a whole new meaning in Atlantis, The Palm hotel's underwater suites. Each room has floor-to-ceiling glass looking into the man-made lagoon filled with 65,000 sea creatures—just don't be shocked when you wake up face-to-face with a shark!

Poppies, Poppies EVERYWHERE

THIS ART INSTALLATION HAD LONDONERS SEEING RED!

LONDON, ENGLAND

IN 2014, A SEA OF RED CERAMIC POPPIES SURROUNDED THE TOWER OF LONDON. The surprising sight was an installation in the tower's moat by artists Paul Cummins and Tom Piper to honor 100 years since the start of Britain's involvement in the First World War. Each poppy—888,246 total—represented a British and Commonwealth individual that died. By the end of the installation's run, about five million people had visited. After it closed, most of the poppies were sold for £25 (nearly U.S. $40) each to raise money for charity. The others will tour the U.K. in a traveling exhibit until 2018, when they'll be put on display at the Imperial War Museums in London and Manchester.

DO YOU
KNOW YOUR
LANDMARKS?

Many countries around the world have unique landmarks that make them stand out from the rest. Do you have any idea where these wacky landmarks are located? Read the clues and then match the description to the country on the map!

PERU **E**

1 CROOKED HOUSE GALLERY

This medieval building, named for its twisty appearance, houses paintings, textiles, sculptures and other pieces of artwork. You'll find it in a country with a queen.

These hills weren't made by ants—they're a naturally occurring (though oddly shaped) phenomenon. You'll find them in a country made up of many islands.

3 CHOCOLATE HILLS

This crater of fire has been burning natural gas underground for more than 40 years. You'll find it in an oil-rich country in central Asia.

2 DARVAZA GAS CRATER

CHAPTER 7

WEIRD
WORLD OF
SPORTS

RODENTS SURF AND SKATE · BUNNIES HOP INT
UM · THE ULTIMATE SLIP 'N' SLIDE · WACKY ROE
DODGEBALL = SERIOUS FUN · INVISIBLE PAINT DE
NTAIN IN EUROPE · WEIRDEST MASCOTS · RECORD

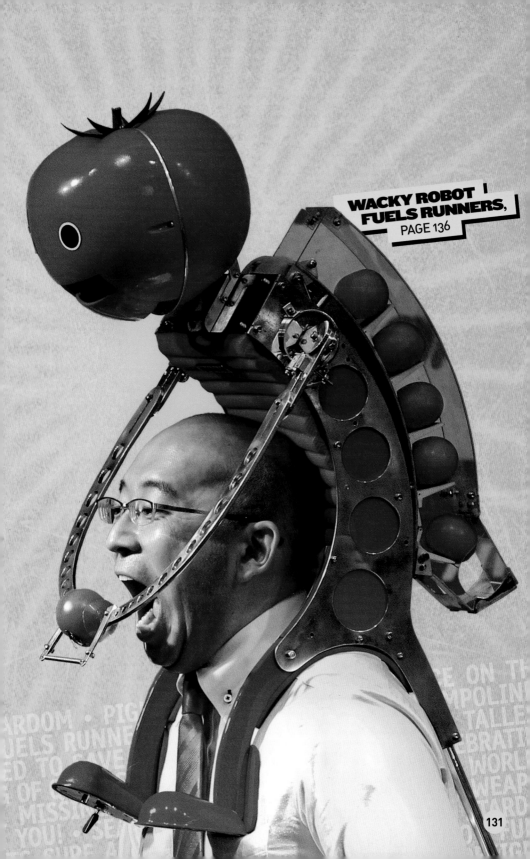

WACKY ROBOT FUELS RUNNERS, PAGE 136

UNUSUAL ANIMAL SPORTS

COWABUNGA!

RAD RODENTS
SURF AND SKATE

A **BABY MOUSE** IS CALLED A **PiNKY.**

GOLD COAST, AUSTRALIA

Shane Willmott's band of "radical rodents" may have the coolest owner ever. These mice aren't running on wheels, they're riding waves and shredding (custom-built) ramps! Willmott became famous for teaching his pets how to surf, and recently he introduced them to skateboarding to keep them busy when the weather turns cold. He insists that mice are naturals, because their bodies sit so low to the ground, and he says they're always ready to get right back on the board. Hang ten, little dudes!

NEWS FEED

>>> CARROLL VALLEY, PENNSYLVANIA, U.S.A.: MEET RATATOUILLE, A SNOW-BOARDING OPOSSUM! WEARING AN ADORABLE SWEATER, THE CURIOUS

BUNNIES
HOP into STARDOM

STOCKHOLM, SWEDEN

You've probably heard of horse jumping competitions—but rabbit jumping? Kaninhop, a scaled-down version of horse jumping for our floppy-eared friends, was invented in Sweden more than 30 years ago. Now bunny-hopping clubs are cropping up all over the world. Trained rabbits compete in a variety of events, including long jump, high jump, and obstacle courses with different size hurdles. Hopefully a carrot is waiting at the end!

WHEN **RABBITS** ARE **HAPPY,** THEY **"BINKY"** BY JUMPING IN THE **AIR** AND **TWISTING** AROUND.

YOU CAN **SWiM** WITH **PIGS** IN THE **TROPICAL WATERS** OFF **THE BAHAMAS.**

PIGLETS COMPETE FOR A PLACE ON THE PODIUM

AND ... THEY'RE OFF!

MOSCOW, RUSSIA

Going for gold isn't just for humans—the porky participants in the Pig Olympics have proven swine can be serious athletes, too. Contestants competed in swimming, racing, and a version of soccer dubbed "pigball," where two teams of pigs chase a ball (covered in fish oil!) toward a goal to score points. Though they started in Russia, the games have also been held in China and the United States. But it's too late to catch this amazing feat of swine. Sadly, the last event took place in 2009.

CRITTER SHREDS THE SLOPES LIKE A PRO—AND JUDGING FROM HIS POPULAR YOUTUBE VIDEO, IT APPEARS HE HAS A GREAT TIME DOING IT.

THE ULTiMATE
SLiP 'N' SLiDE

EXTREME SPORT FEATURES THRILLS AND CH-CH-CHILLS!

ALTESCH GLACIER, SWITZERLAND

IT'S FUN, IT'S FAST, IT'S OUTRAGEOUSLY DANGEROUS ... it's glacier boarding, a new sport thrill seekers are sure to love. Glacier boarding—which typically involves riding a Boogie board down ice-cold channels carved into melting glaciers—requires a wet suit, flippers, helmet, plenty of training, and more than a little luck. Boarders face risks like getting caught in freezing floods and being hit with falling ice. No wonder the popular energy drink company Red Bull gave it an "insanity level" of 8 out of 10! This potentially short-lived sport may end up like glacier surfing—riding a wave made by glacier ice falling into the ocean—which a couple of surfers tried in 2007 before ultimately deciding it was much too dangerous to ever attempt again!

WACKY **ROBOT** *FUELS* RUNNERS— WITH TOMATOES!

TOKYO, JAPAN

Some runners prefer protein-packed snacks when hunger hits, but one competitor in the 2015 Tokyo Marathon opted for something different: tomatoes. This 18-pound (8-kg) robot piggybacks on the runner—who pushes a small lever on the foot to receive a mouthful of tomato. Though it may have been a publicity stunt by the Japanese tomato juice and ketchup maker that created it, tomatoes do contain nutrients that help fight fatigue!

MMM ... TOMATOES!

KID CLIMBER SCALES TALLEST MOUNTAIN IN EUROPE

WHO TYLER ARMSTRONG

WHAT AT THE AGE OF 11, CLIMBED RUSSIA'S 18,510-FOOT (5,642-M) MOUNT ELBRUS, THE THIRD MOUNTAIN IN HIS ATTEMPT TO REACH THE TOP OF THE HIGHEST PEAK ON EACH CONTINENT.

WHEN 2015

WHY ARMSTRONG IS CLIMBING HIGH FOR A GOOD CAUSE: TO RAISE MONEY FOR DUCHENNE MUSCULAR DYSTROPHY. HE CLIMBED

MOUNT KILIMANJARO (AFRICA) IN 2012, MOUNT ACONCAGUA (SOUTH AMERICA) IN 2013, AND PLANS TO SUMMIT MOUNT EVEREST (ASIA) IN 2016 AND DENALI (NORTH AMERICA) IN 2017.

NEWS FEED

>>> **VARIOUS LOCATIONS:** GET YOUR BEST ZOMBIE MOVES READY. EVERY OCTOBER, MICHAEL JACKSON FANS FORM LARGE GROUPS AROUND THE GLOBE FOR

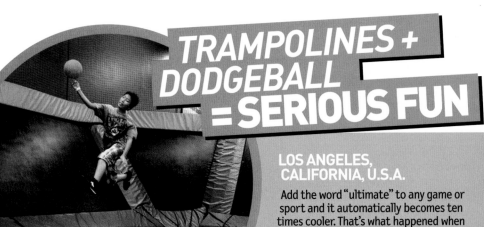

TRAMPOLINES + DODGEBALL = SERIOUS FUN

LOS ANGELES, CALIFORNIA, U.S.A.

Add the word "ultimate" to any game or sport and it automatically becomes ten times cooler. That's what happened when Sky Zone Trampoline Parks created ultimate dodgeball—a game with rules similar to regular dodgeball, except players compete on trampoline courts. The springy surface allows participants to jump over balls and throw from up to ten feet (3 m) in the air!

INVISIBLE PAINT — DESIGNED TO SAVE LIVES

GOTHENBURG, SWEDEN

Carmaker Volvo collaborated with a Swedish start-up to create LifePaint: spray-on paint for bikes that's invisible in daylight but is super reflective at night. The temporary coating washes off in about a week. Volvo gave away a bunch of cans in 2015 to kick-start their safety campaign, and they're hoping the practical product will be successful enough to take off internationally.

THRILL THE WORLD, AN INTERNATIONAL MASS DANCE PARTY CELEBRATING THE POP STAR'S FAMOUS HORROR SONG "THRILLER."

ABU DHABI, UNITED ARAB EMIRATES YAS MARINA CIRCUIT MASCOTS—TWO ROBOTS ... ER, CARTOON DRIVERS?—HANG OUT NEAR THE TRACK DURING THE FORMULA ONE WORLD CHAMPIONSHIP.

[WEIRDEST MASCOTS]

Team mascots make cheering more fun—especially when they're as unique as these colorful characters. Root, root, root for the home team with the world's weirdest mascots!

STANFORD, CALIFORNIA, U.S.A. WITH NO OFFICIAL MASCOT TO REPRESENT THE SCHOOL, STANFORD'S TREE—A MEMBER OF THE STANFORD BAND—FILLS IN FOR THE JOB.

THE MASCOT FOR THE **TORONTO BLUE JAYS** WAS ONCE *EJECTED FROM A GAME* FOR GETTING THE CROWD RILED OVER A **BAD UMP CALL.**

PASADENA, CALIFORNIA, U.S.A. SUPER FROG, THE HORNED FROG MASCOT FROM TEXAS CHRISTIAN UNIVERSITY, CELEBRATES HIS SCHOOL'S ROSE BOWL VICTORY.

IN ENGLAND,
SOCCER TEAM
MASCOTS COMPETE
IN AN **ANNUAL**
HURDLiNG RACE.

LONDON, ENGLAND WENLOCK, ONE OF TWO MADE-UP CHARACTERS FOR THE 2012 OLYMPIC GAMES, POSES WITH SPRINTER USAIN BOLT.

GREENSBORO, NORTH CAROLINA, U.S.A. WUSHOCK, THE WICHITA STATE SHOCKERS' MASCOT (A BUNDLE OF WHEAT), CHEERS ON THE MEN'S BASKETBALL TEAM.

NEW ORLEANS, LOUISIANA, U.S.A. FORMER ARENA FOOTBALL LEAGUE MASCOT BONES THE SKELETON KEPT WATCH OVER HIS NEW ORLEANS VOODOO TEAM.

SANTA CRUZ, CALIFORNIA, U.S.A. UNIVERSITY OF CALIFORNIA AT SANTA CRUZ'S MASCOT, SAMMY THE BANANA SLUG, IS ALWAYS UP FOR THE CELEBRATION.

RECORD

FURMAN ATTEMPTED TO BREAK THE WORLD RECORD FOR JUGGLING UNDERWATER CONTINUOUSLY IN AN AQUARIUM IN KUALA LUMPUR, MALAYSIA. UNFORTUNATELY, IT WASN'T HIS DAY.

CHECK OUT THOSE COLORFUL KICKS! FURMAN WORE THEM WHEN HE BROKE THE WORLD RECORD FOR THE HEAVIEST SHOES WALKED IN, AT 323 POUNDS (146.5 KG)!

KING

MEET THE GUY WHO HOLDS THE RECORD FOR HOLDING THE MOST RECORDS

QUEENS, NEW YORK, U.S.A.

Most people have never broken a world record—Ashrita Furman has broken nearly 600. Although he wasn't athletic as a kid, Furman says he was competitive. He began his quest to hold the most records after he started studying meditation, which he says gave him so much energy he had to find a positive outlet for it.

Furman set his first record in 1979, when he completed 27,000 jumping jacks without stopping! Nearly 40 years later, he's broken a Guinness World Record on every continent, including completing the fastest mile on a pogo stick in Antarctica. He most enjoys setting records around the world while weaving in elements of local culture. He once set a record in Colombia for being the fastest to blow a postage stamp 100 meters (almost 110 yards)—which he did while holding a sloth, an animal native to South America, even though Guinness didn't recognize the sloth as part of the record.

For Furman, breaking a record is as much about thinking outside the box to solve a problem as it is about the athletic achievement. "They always say the journey is the reward," he says. "And I find that's true for the records." But, he adds, "You have to choose something you love, because you're going to spend a lot of time practicing!"

PUCKER UP SOCCER PLAYER LAURENT BLANC KISSED TEAMMATE (AND GOALKEEPER) FABIEN BARTHEZ'S BALD HEAD BEFORE EACH SOCCER GAME.

SMACK!

[SPORTY **SUPERSTITIONS**]

What wacky rituals get you geared up for the game? These professional athletes' superstitions have them bouncing, kissing, and dunking their way to victory!

SLAP CHAP FOOTBALL PLAYER JOHN HENDERSON'S PREGAME WARM-UP INVOLVED HAVING HIS COACH SLAP HIM IN THE FACE!

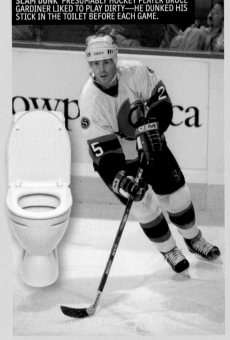

SLAM DUNK PRESUMABLY HOCKEY PLAYER BRUCE GARDINER LIKED TO PLAY DIRTY—HE DUNKED HIS STICK IN THE TOILET BEFORE EACH GAME.

IN BETWEEN POINTS, **TENNIS STAR RAFAEL NADAL** ALWAYS **CROSSES** THE **LINES** ON **COURT** WITH HIS **RIGHT FOOT.**

1, 2, 3...

BOUNCE THAT BALL
TENNIS PLAYER SERENA WILLIAMS WINS BY BOUNCING THE BALL FIVE TIMES BEFORE HER FIRST SERVE AND TWICE BEFORE THE SECOND ONE. SHE ALSO HAS TO TIE HER SHOES A CERTAIN WAY AND WEARS THE SAME SOCKS THROUGHOUT A TOURNAMENT.

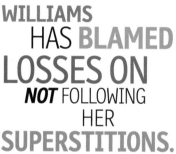

WILLIAMS HAS BLAMED LOSSES ON *NOT* FOLLOWING HER SUPERSTITIONS.

THREE IS A MAGIC NUMBER
BASEBALL PLAYER LARRY WALKER LOVES THE NUMBER THREE SO MUCH THAT HIS TEAM NUMBER WAS ALWAYS 33, HE GOT MARRIED AT 3:33 ON NOVEMBER 3, AND HIS 1993 CONTRACT WITH THE EXPOS WAS FOR $3 MILLION.

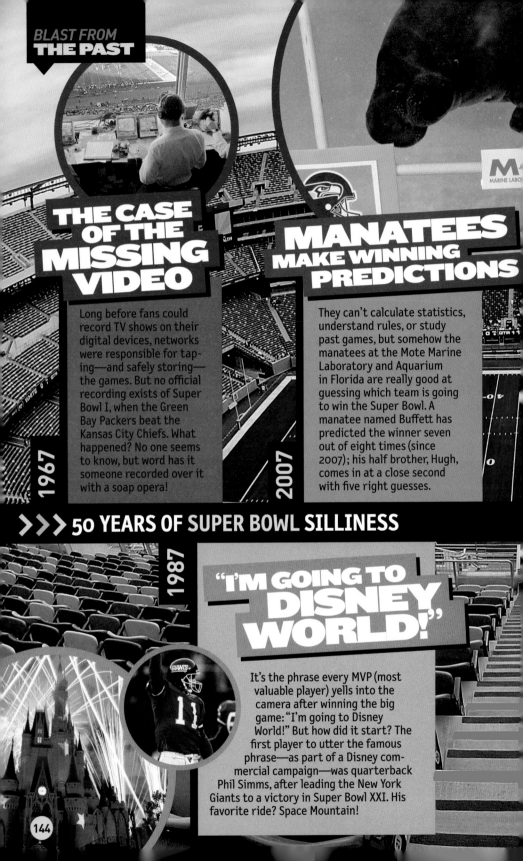

THE CASE OF THE MISSING VIDEO

1967

Long before fans could record TV shows on their digital devices, networks were responsible for taping—and safely storing—the games. But no official recording exists of Super Bowl I, when the Green Bay Packers beat the Kansas City Chiefs. What happened? No one seems to know, but word has it someone recorded over it with a soap opera!

MANATEES MAKE WINNING PREDICTIONS

2007

They can't calculate statistics, understand rules, or study past games, but somehow the manatees at the Mote Marine Laboratory and Aquarium in Florida are really good at guessing which team is going to win the Super Bowl. A manatee named Buffett has predicted the winner seven out of eight times (since 2007); his half brother, Hugh, comes in at a close second with five right guesses.

>>> 50 YEARS OF SUPER BOWL SILLINESS

1987

"I'M GOING TO DISNEY WORLD!"

It's the phrase every MVP (most valuable player) yells into the camera after winning the big game: "I'm going to Disney World!" But how did it start? The first player to utter the famous phrase—as part of a Disney commercial campaign—was quarterback Phil Simms, after leading the New York Giants to a victory in Super Bowl XXI. His favorite ride? Space Mountain!

NO SEATS FOR YOU!

2011

It was like a very disappointing game of musical chairs: 400 Super Bowl XLV ticket holders were left without seats to sit in. A section of the Texas stadium's temporary seats weren't finished in time, so 850 of the 1,250 fans that were supposed to be seated there ended up in other seats. The rest were offered a refund worth three times their ticket price! Understandably, the fans were still pretty upset, even though the NFL offered them (standing-room) viewing spots from other places in the stadium.

BESIDES **THANKSGIVING,** AMERICANS **EAT MORE FOOD** ON **SUPER BOWL SUNDAY** THAN **ANY OTHER DAY** OF THE YEAR.

SEATTLE'S SECRET (AND COLORFUL) WEAPON

2015

Running back Marshawn Lynch of the Seattle Seahawks—the team that won Super Bowl XLVIII and was the runner-up in Super Bowl XLIX—has a sweet game-time tradition: Skittles. Lynch started eating the rainbow-colored candy as a kid before games, and they're still part of his pregame ritual. Skittles even released a special Super Bowl XLIX version of the candies coated in green and blue, the Seahawks' team colors.

OVER **200 MILLION SKITTLES** CANDIES ARE **MADE EVERY DAY.**

145

MONSTER FiGHT!

BOSTON, MASSACHUSETTS, U.S.A.

RUN FOR YOUR LIVES! *Kaiju*—a Japanese word that means "strange creature" or "monster"—is a genre of movies and entertainment dating back to the 1930s (think Godzilla and his rivals). Now, Kaiju Big Battel is a U.S.-based group that puts crazy made-up monsters (which are really just people wearing costumes) in a wrestling ring and lets them duke it out, making it perhaps the weirdest sport ever! Here, rogue six-eyed sea monster Call-Me-Kevin—a former alien kelp farmer turned poorly trained Big Battel contender with a fondness for pranks—aims to pummel his opponent, a feral beast named the Grudyin.

147

BiZARRE
SPORTS RULES

Think football and rugby are hard to understand?
You're not alone. But they're not the only sports with a long list of wacky rules and crazy customs. Match the rule below to the sport above to see if you can play along with the best of them!

RACE WALKING

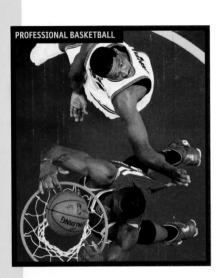

PROFESSIONAL BASKETBALL

BEACH VOLLEYBALL

1.
PLAYERS CAN BE SUSPENDED FOR LEAVING THE BENCH.

2.
IF THE BALL TOUCHES A CERTAIN PLAYER'S HELMET, IT'S A PENALTY.

3.
PLAYERS CHOOSE STAGE NAMES AND WEAR COSTUMES.

4.
IF PLAYERS CUT IN LINE FOR THEIR TURN, THEY'RE AUTOMATICALLY OUT FOR THAT ROUND.

GOLF

CRICKET

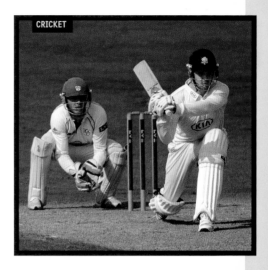

PROFESSIONAL BASEBALL

ROLLER DERBY

"RINK RASH" IS THE **NAME** FOR THE **BURNS** AND **BRUISES** ACQUIRED DURING A **ROLLER DERBY** GAME.

5.
IF OPPOSING TEAMS SHOW UP WEARING THE SAME COLOR, A COIN TOSS WILL DECIDE WHO HAS TO CHANGE.

6.
PLAYERS HAVE TO KEEP ONE FOOT ON THE GROUND AT ALL TIMES.

7.
FANS ARE REQUIRED TO STAY QUIET, NOT CHEER, WHEN THEIR FAVORITE PLAYER IS UP.

ANSWERS: 1. PROFESSIONAL BASKETBALL, 2. CRICKET, 3. ROLLER DERBY, 4. PROFESSIONAL BASEBALL, 5. BEACH VOLLEYBALL, 6. RACE WALKING, 7. GOLF

149

CHAPTER 8

CULTURE SHOCK

"THE WORLD'S FASTEST HOT TUB"

CADILLAC
OF CARPOOLS,
PAGE 152

Carpool De Ville

"GHOST SHIP" LIGHTS UP AMSTERDAM CANAL

AMSTERDAM, THE NETHERLANDS

A famous ship called the *Flying Dutchman*—part of seafaring folklore since the 17th century—seemed to appear out of thin air over the Amsterdam Canal at the city's 2014 Light Festival. Architecture group VisualSKIN created the supercool optical illusion using water, lights, and projectors to cast the ghostly, 3-D image over the canal. The spookiest part? When the wind picked up, the boat began to bob and sway as if it were sailing through the water!

THE CADILLAC OF CARPOOLS

SWEET RIDE

WHO ENGINEERS (AND PALS) DUNCAN FORSTER AND PHIL WEICKER

WHAT BUILT A HOT TUB IN THE BACK OF A CADILLAC!

WHERE LOS ANGELES, CALIFORNIA, U.S.A.

HOW TO CREATE A FULLY FUNCTIONAL HOT TUB ON WHEELS, PALS FORSTER AND WEICKER COMPLETELY STRIPPED THE CAR'S INTERIOR. THEN THEY ADDED SUPPORT TO HOLD THE EXTRA WATER WEIGHT, LINED THE INSIDE WITH FIBERGLASS, AND WATERPROOFED THE CAR'S CONTROLS. THE ENGINE NOT ONLY MOVES THE CAR, IT ALSO HEATS THE WATER TO A STEAMY 102°F (39°C).

NEWS FEED

>>> **FRANCE:** THE MAKERS OF MONOPOLY HAVE RELEASED A SPECIAL EDITION OF THE POPULAR BOARD GAME IN FRANCE THAT INCLUDES REAL CASH. EIGHT

GIANT DOLLS
ON PARADE

PERTH, AUSTRALIA

They're alive! Larger-than-life marionette puppets took to the streets of Perth for the 2015 International Arts Festival. They may look like Pinocchio's long-lost relatives, but the dolls were designed to tell a story about Western Australia's history. It took a team of more than 300 volunteers to maneuver the marionettes—a 20-foot (6-m)-tall girl and a scuba diver nearly twice that size—through the city.

AHOY, MATEY!

SHIPWRECKED
LEGO PIECES
COME ASHORE

CORNWALL, ENGLAND

Twenty years ago, a rogue wave sent a shipping container holding more than four million Lego pieces overboard off the coast of Cornwall. Remarkably, pieces are still washing up on Cornish shores today! Treasure hunters of all ages have been combing the beaches for the toys—things like scuba gear, octopuses, and dragons. It's become quite competitive: People even post their discoveries and trade their finds online.

LUCKY SETS—INCLUDING ONE WORTH 20,580 EUROS (U.S. $22,366)—ARE HIDDEN AMONG 30,000 GAMES.

MAY THE
FROST BE

SAPPORO, JAPAN

Snowy Sapporo is a magical place in the winter, especially in February when the town hosts an annual snow festival. Every year since 1950, huge sculptures have been made from snow and ice, but some say the coolest (or at least most galactic) entry in 2014 was this *Star Wars*–themed sculpture standing 49 feet (15 m) tall. It took 400 troops from Japan's Ground Self-Defense Force 11th Brigade a whole month and 3,500 tons (3,175 MT) of snow to complete. There have been plenty of awesome sculptures in the past—dragons, cities, cartoon characters, and thousands of little snowmen—but only one featuring Darth Vader!

WITH YOU

STAR WARS CHARACTERS TAKE OVER THE SAPPORO SNOW FESTIVAL

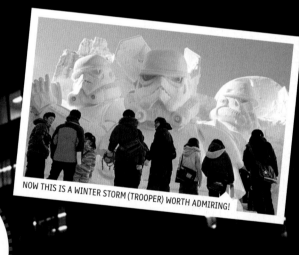

NOW THIS IS A WINTER STORM (TROOPER) WORTH ADMIRING!

FESTIVAL-GOERS CAN **RIDE DOWN** A **39**-FOOT (12-M) **SLIDE** CARVED FROM **ICE.**

THE AMOUNT OF **SNOW** *USED TO BUILD* ALL THE FESTIVAL'S **SCULPTURES** COULD FILL **65,000** PICKUP TRUCKS!

LIBRARIES
YOU MUST
SEE TO BELIEVE

YE OLDE BOOKSHOPPE

SOUTH SINAI, EGYPT

Ever wonder what the oldest continually running library in the world looks like? A lot like a sand castle, it turns out. St. Catherine's Monastery, a nearly 1,500-year-old holy site, holds thousands of religious, educational, and crazy cool first-edition books. In 2013 and 2014, the monastery had to temporarily shutter due to security concerns in Egypt. But book lovers weren't the only ones sad about this—the nearby town relies on tourists' bucks to survive. Thank goodness St. Catherine's is back to being open for business!

BEN FRANKLIN HELPED START **THE FIRST** *LENDING* **LIBRARY** IN THE **U.S.**

NEWS FEED

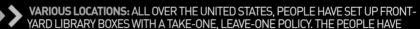

VARIOUS LOCATIONS: ALL OVER THE UNITED STATES, PEOPLE HAVE SET UP FRONT-YARD LIBRARY BOXES WITH A TAKE-ONE, LEAVE-ONE POLICY. THE PEOPLE HAVE

THE U.S. *LIBRARY OF CONGRESS,* THE WORLD'S BIGGEST LIBRARY, HAS **838** MILES OF *BOOKSHELVES.*
(1,349 KM)

PICTURE THIS!

IWAKI, JAPAN

Kids rule at the Picture Book Museum—a bright, modern library designed with preschoolers in mind. The outside may be a simple concrete building, but the inside is brimming with books and crowded with color. Famous architect Tadao Ando had only one stipulation—the founder wanted to see the book covers—which inspired the quirky design. He filled the interior with little cubbyholes that hold each book so the cover faces outward. The library has about 10,000 books, but don't think you have to get through all those in one sitting: Only 1,500 are on display at a time.

THE **WORLD'S LARGEST** *LIBRARY FINE* EVER PAID WAS **$345.14** ON A **47**-YEARS-OVERDUE BOOK OF *POETRY* IN 2002.

ROOFTOP LIBRARY LOUNGE

DELFT, THE NETHERLANDS

At first look, Delft University of Technology's library lawn looks like any other grassy knoll—until you realize that the shelves of books are actually housed underneath! The slanted living roof was designed as a recreation space, punctuated by the concrete cone that rises up through the lawn from the library below. And though reading and lounging are absolutely encouraged, there are some rules to follow: No skiing, sledding, or cycling allowed.

GOOD INTENTIONS, BUT A FEW ANGRY NEIGHBORS HAVE MADE A STINK, SAYING THE BOXES BREAK CITY CODES AND FORCING MANY OF THEM TO BE TAKEN DOWN.

LITTLE TOY CRITIC

EVAN AND HIS SISTER DIP INTO DESSERT WITH THE DIPPIN' DOTS FROZEN DOT MAKER.

SO FAR, EVAN'S **FAVORITE** TOY HAS BEEN THE *LEGO* **STAR WARS** **DEATH STAR.**

EVAN STARTS FROM SCRATCH WITH A LEGO DIMENSIONS SET.

HiTS ^THE BiG-TiME

THIS YOUTUBE CELEBRITY IS A KID JUST LIKE YOU!

NORTHERN CALIFORNIA, U.S.A.

In many ways, ten-year-old Evan is a normal kid: He loves putting together Lego sets, playing Minecraft, doing karate, and wants to be a video game designer or artist when he grows up. But Evan already has an awesome job: He reviews toys for a living!

Evan and his dad, Jared, run Evan-TubeHD, a hugely popular YouTube channel they started in 2011 that now has more than two million subscribers. Jared films Evan as he opens, puts together, and plays with all kinds of cool toys. The family now makes enough money through advertising on EvanTubeHD that both Evan and his younger sister have big savings accounts for when they're older.

Now that Evan has achieved Internet fame, toy companies are clamoring for his reviews. His dad says they get so many free toys that they don't even have time to open them all! They send the unopened toys to charities like Toys for Tots and Goodwill, and opened toys go to local schools, church groups, and families in need—once Evan and his sister are done playing with them, of course!

What's the neatest part about being an Internet celebrity? "People always stop me to say hi," Evan says. "I also got to be on TV and in a commercial."

I'M TRYING!

HUMANKIND'S
FIRST MAKEUP

3500 B.C.

Ancient Egyptians were rocking the smoky black eyeliner look way before it debuted on modern runways and in fashion magazines. In fact, they started smearing kohl—a ground-up mineral mixed with liquid and all sorts of other ingredients—on their eyelids thousands of years ago. The ancient trend was part fashion, part function: The kohl helped keep the desert sand, sun, and flies out of their eyes!

SUCK IT IN!

1800s

Corsets were a way for women to create an hourglass figure. Ladies used these supertight lace-up undergarments to reduce their waist size by up to four inches (10 cm). Some people say corsets were dangerous, because they caused the wearers' organs to squish together, but they weren't really any more hazardous than some of today's fashion trends (wearing high heels is no picnic!).

>>> FASHION FORWARD OR FASHION FLOP?

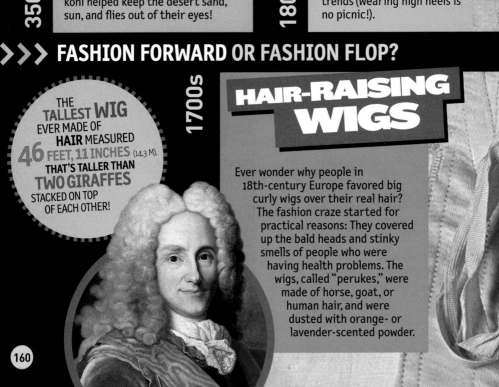

THE TALLEST **WIG** EVER MADE OF **HAIR** MEASURED **46** FEET, 11 INCHES (14.3 M). **THAT'S TALLER THAN TWO GIRAFFES** STACKED ON TOP OF EACH OTHER!

1700s

HAIR-RAISING WIGS

Ever wonder why people in 18th-century Europe favored big curly wigs over their real hair? The fashion craze started for practical reasons: They covered up the bald heads and stinky smells of people who were having health problems. The wigs, called "perukes," were made of horse, goat, or human hair, and were dusted with orange- or lavender-scented powder.

THESE BOOTS WERE MADE FOR DANCING

2010s

These aren't pointe shoes—the kind ballerinas wear—but rather pointy boots, the kind made popular recently by men who listen to "musica tribal," a new type of music that's taken off in Mexico. Folks started wearing the boots to dance competitions, extending the crazy curls at the end of these awesomely colorful boots in an attempt to one-up each other. Now some of them reach as high as the wearer's waist!

ALL DOLLED UP

1990s

Japan has premiered plenty of wacky street fashions over the years, but the Lolita craze—with its puffy dresses, lacy bonnets, and pastel-colored parasols—popularized in the 1990s has caught on in other parts of the world. It's an extremely frilly look (and one with a lot of layers!). Love it or hate it, there's no denying it's very *kawaii*, or "cute" in Japanese.

TiNY TOWNS

MARVELOUS MINIATURES CREATE STORYBOOK SCENES

ANKARA, TURKEY

An art director and motion graphic designer by day, Ali Alamedy has a very unusual hobby: building super-detailed—but extremely scaled-down—scenes called dioramas. The artist, who was born in Baghdad, Iraq, had been dreaming of these projects since he was a kid, but he didn't actually begin building them until he became an adult. He didn't even know the term "diorama" existed!

"My mother taught me to read and write at the age of five, and I've been reading novels and other books since then," Alamedy says. "Reading so many books enhanced my imagination and helped me a lot when I started with miniatures. It was like I was traveling to the locations of the stories, living the adventures of its heroes, and feeling all the environments!"

Although his sculptures look real, he's never actually visited the cities he creates in his scenes, including Havana, Paris, London, and New York. He loves best the views that look kind of rusty and old "because those effects mean the cities have witnessed many events."

How can you make these amazing miniatures at home? Alamedy suggests not letting yourself get hung up on finding the perfect materials. Use what you have around the house: paper clips, foam board, coffee grounds, foil, etc. But whatever you do, "Keep doing what you love," he says. "And be creative in how to use things to meet your needs."

THE WORD "DIORAMA" MEANS "THROUGH THAT WHICH IS SEEN."

IN 2015, MINECRAFT FANS IN ENGLAND MADE A **DIORAMA OF** *LEGO PIECES* THAT COVERED **184** SQUARE FEET (17.1 SQ M).

THE CITY LOOKS TINY COMPARED TO ALAMEDY'S OLDEST SON!

A TEENSY PLAYROOM BETTER SUITED FOR A BUG THAN A BABY.

163

BERRY BIG BLAST

[EXPLODING ART]

Photographer Alan Sailer likes to shoot his subjects—literally! He launches pellets and marbles at food, toys, and other objects, and then takes photos of the explosion with an ultra high-speed flash. Check it out!

WRECKED RUBIK'S CUBE

EXPLOSION OF COLOR

A NORMAL
PHOTOGRAPHIC FLASH IS
1/1000 OF A SECOND.
SAILER'S IS
1/1,000,000.

EGG-STRAORDINARILY MESSY

M&BAM!

POP GOES THE POPSICLE

FIRECRACKER MEETS MARBLE

Mother Nature's Concerto

AWESOME ARCHITECTURE MAKES MUSIC OUT OF RAIN

DRESDEN, GERMANY

WHAT IF RAINSTORMS CREATED BEAUTIFUL SYMPHONIES OUTSIDE YOUR WINDOW? Wet weather might not bother you at all! Three artists in Germany set out to do just that by creating a weirdly wonderful project that turns raindrops into rhapsodies. Inspired by the various-size rainspouts and bizarre architecture in St. Petersburg, Russia, the "rain theatre" was born. The maze of metal cones and pipes funnels water off the roof the same as any rain gutter would, but the intricate design acts like an instrument as well. Now instead of dashing inside to stay dry, people love to stop, stare, and listen to the rain.

HEAD, SHOULDERS, KNEES AND TOES, KNEES AND TOES!

Grab your friends to play this WACKY GAME of mix-and-match BODY PARTS.

Draw inspiration from some of the fun characters in this chapter!
- The giant marionettes from Perth
- Pirates from Amsterdam's ghost ship
- Darth Vader or the Stormtroopers from Sapporo's snow sculpture
- Crazy fashion finds on pages 160–161

What you'll need:
- One rectangular piece of paper, folded into thirds widthwise ("hamburger-style")
- Crayons, markers, or colored pencils
- Two friends to play with

STEP 1:

PLAYER ONE TAKES THE PAPER AND DRAWS A HEAD ON THE TOP THIRD OF THE FOLDED PIECE OF PAPER. USE YOUR IMAGINATION: ADD DETAILS LIKE HAIR, GLASSES, HATS, BEARDS, ETC. FOLD THE PAPER SO THAT YOU CAN'T SEE YOUR DRAWING, AND HAND THE PAPER TO PLAYER TWO.

HELPFUL HINT:
Draw just enough over the fold so that the next player's drawing will match up with yours.

STEP 2:

PLAYER TWO THEN DRAWS THE BODY— SHOULDERS, ARMS, CRAZY CLOTHING— BEFORE FOLDING THAT PART DOWN AND HANDING THE REMAINING BLANK THIRD OF PAPER TO PLAYER THREE.

STEP 3:

PLAYER THREE DRAWS THE LEGS AND SHOES. NOW, ALL THREE PLAYERS GATHER AROUND TO UNVEIL THE FINISHED ARTWORK: UNFOLD THE PAPER AND GET READY TO LAUGH AT THE CRAZY PERSON YOU'VE CREATED!

INDEX

CREDITS

The publisher would like to thank the following people for their help in creating this book: Ashlee Brown, project editor; Chelsea Lin and Alison Stevens, writers; Julie Beer and Michelle Harris, researchers; and Danny Meldung and Margaret Sidlosky, photo researchers.

Since 1888, the National Geographic Society has funded more than 12,000 research, exploration, and preservation projects around the world. The Society receives funds from National Geographic Partners, LLC, funded in part by your purchase. A portion of the proceeds from this book supports this vital work. To learn more, visit www.natgeo.com/info.

NATIONAL GEOGRAPHIC and Yellow Border Design are trademarks of the National Geographic Society, used under license.

For more information, please visit nationalgeographic.com, call 1-800-647-5463, or write to the following address:
National Geographic Partners
1145 17th Street N.W.
Washington, D.C. 20036-4688 U.S.A.

Visit us online at nationalgeographic.com/books

For librarians and teachers: ngchildrensbooks.org

More for kids from National Geographic:
kids.nationalgeographic.com

For information about special discounts for bulk purchases, please contact National Geographic Books Special Sales: ngspecsales@ngs.org

For rights or permissions inquiries, please contact National Geographic Books Subsidiary Rights: ngbookrights@ngs.org

Paperback ISBN: 978-1-4263-2421-5
Reinforced Library Binding ISBN: 978-1-4263-2422-2

Art Directed by James Hiscott, Jr.
Designed by Dawn McFadin

Printed in the United States of America
16/QGT-RRDML/1